PORTUGUESE STUDIES

VOLUME 34 NUMBER 1
2018

Portugal, Forty-Four Years after the Revolution

Founding Editor
HELDER MACEDO

Guest Editor
SEBASTIÁN ROYO

Editors
CATARINA FOUTO
TOBY GREEN
TORI HOLMES
PAULO DE MEDEIROS
PAUL MELO E CASTRO
HILARY OWEN
CLAIRE WILLIAMS

Editorial Assistant
RICHARD CORRELL

Production Editor
GRAHAM NELSON

MODERN HUMANITIES RESEARCH ASSOCIATION

PORTUGUESE STUDIES

A peer-reviewed biannual multi-disciplinary journal devoted to research on the cultures, literatures, history and societies of the Lusophone world

International Advisory Board

David Brookshaw
João de Pina Cabral
Ivo José de Castro
Thomas F. Earle
John Gledson
Anna Klobucka

Maria Manuel Lisboa
Kenneth Maxwell
Laura de Mello e Souza
Maria Irene Ramalho
Silviano Santiago

Portuguese Studies and other journals published by the MHRA may be ordered from Turpin Distribution (http://ebiz.turpin-distribution.com/).

The **Modern Humanities Research Association** was founded in Cambridge in 1918 and has become an international organization with members in all parts of the world. It is a registered charity number 1064670, and a company limited by guarantee, registered in England number 3446016. Its main object is to encourage advanced study and research in modern and medieval European languages, literatures, and cultures by its publication of journals, book series, and its Style Guide. Further information about the activities of the Association and individual membership may be obtained from the Membership Secretary, email membership@mhra.org.uk, or from the website at: www.mhra.org.uk

Disclaimer: Statements of fact and opinion in the content of *Portuguese Studies* are those of the respective authors and contributors and not of the journal editors or of the Modern Humanities Research Association (MHRA). MHRA makes no representation, express or implied, in respect of the accuracy of the material in this journal and cannot accept any legal responsibility or liability for any errors or omissions that may be made.

Parts of this work may be reproduced as permitted under legal provisions for fair dealing (or fair use) for the purposes of research, private study, criticism, or review, or when a relevant collective licensing agreement is in place. All other reproduction requires the written permission of the copyright holder who may be contacted at rights@mhra.org.uk.

ISSN 0267–5315 (print) ISSN 2222–4270 (online)
ISBN 978-1-78188-751-6

© 2018 The Modern Humanities Research Association
Salisbury House, Station Road, Cambridge CB1 2LA, United Kingdom

Portuguese Studies vol. 34 no. 1

Portugal, Forty-Four Years after the Revolution

CONTENTS

Introduction: Portugal, Forty-Four Years after the Revolution Sebastián Royo	5
What 25 April Was and Why It Mattered Robert M. Fishman	20
Constitution-Making and the Democratization of Portugal: An Enduring Legacy António Costa Pinto	35
The Cooperative Movement in Portugal beyond the Revolution: Housing Cooperatives between Shifting Tides Camila Rodrigues and Tiago Fernandes	52
The Portuguese Presidencies of the European Union: A Preliminary Study Nuno Severiano Teixeira and Reinaldo Saraiva Hermenegildo	70
The Legacies of Revolution: Path-Dependence and Economic Performance in Portugal Sebastián Royo	86
Portugal's Social and Labour Market Policy: The Crisis, the Troika and Beyond Miguel Glatzer	104
Reviews	119
Abstracts	133

NOTES FOR CONTRIBUTORS

Articles to be considered for publication may be on any subject within the field but must not exceed 7,500 words, and should be submitted in a form ready for publication in English, sent as an email attachment to the Editorial Assistant at portuguese@mhra.org.uk.

Contributions whose standard of English is inadequate will be returned. Any quotations in Portuguese must be accompanied by an English translation. Submissions in Portuguese may be considered, but publication will be conditional on provision of a satisfactory translation at the author's expense. The Editorial Assistant may undertake translations on request for a reasonable charge.

Text and references should conform precisely to the conventions of the *MHRA Style Guide*, 3rd edn, 2013 (978-1-78188-009-8), £9.50, $19.00, €12.00, obtainable in print or online version from www.style.mhra.org.uk. All articles are subject to independent, anonymous peer review by experts in the field; authors receive written feedback on the editors' decision and guidance on any revisions required. *Portuguese Studies* regrets it must charge contributors for the cost of corrections in proof deemed excessive.

It is a condition of publication in this journal that authors of articles and reviews assign copyright, including electronic copyright, to the MHRA. Inter alia, this allows the General Editor to deal efficiently and consistently with requests from third parties for permission to reproduce material. The journal has been published simultaneously in printed and electronic form since January 2001. Permission, without fee, for authors to use their own material in other publications, after a reasonable period of time has elapsed, is not normally withheld. Authors may make closed-access deposit of accepted manuscripts in their academic institution's digital repository upon acceptance. Full open access to the accepted manuscript is permitted no sooner than 12 months following publication of the Contribution by the MHRA. Contributions may also be republished on authors' personal websites without seeking further permission from the Association, but no earlier than 12 months after publication by the MHRA.

Books for review should be sent to: Reviews Editor, *Portuguese Studies*, Dr Paul Melo e Castro, School of Languages, Cultures, and Societies, University of Leeds, Leeds LS2 9JT.

Introduction: Portugal, Forty-Four Years after the Revolution

Sebastián Royo

Suffolk University, Boston, MA

The year 2018 marks the forty-fourth anniversary of the Portuguese Revolution. After decades of relative isolation under an authoritarian regime, the success of the democratic transition paved the way for full membership of the European Community in 1986. The combined processes of democratization and European integration have shaped the country's development during the last four decades, and to this day they are still crucial in policy-making and policy outcomes. This special volume reflects on the legacies of the revolution, and seeks to examine Portugal's transformation over the last four decades.

The pattern of Portuguese history has been described, crudely, as a graph shaped like an upside-down V. The graph rises, bumpily at times, through 600 years under the Romans, 700 years or so partly under the Moors, and a century of empire-building, to the peak of Portuguese power in the sixteenth century. The discovery of the largest gold deposits in South America at the end of the seventeenth century led to the Brazilian gold rush, with hundreds of thousands of Portuguese moving to the region to seek their fortune. After that, though, the riches of the American and African colonies were squandered in wars and a vast empire was gradually lost, leaving Portugal poor and powerless. The years following the assassination of the king in 1908 and the subsequent overturn of the monarchy were a period of political chaos, which led to forty years of authoritarian rule under Salazar and Caetano. After the 1974 Carnation Revolution, however, the line on the graph turned upward again. The democratic transition was turbulent and included a revolutionary period, but it culminated in the establishment of a parliamentary democracy. These developments were followed by the progressive return of the country to the international arena — having been relatively isolated during the dictatorship — bringing a new era of modernity.

The purpose of this special volume is to reflect on the legacies of the revolutionary transition and examine what has happened in the country during the last four decades. The articles identify the basic changes in the economy and society of Portugal that occurred as a result of the democratization process. They also assess the impact that these changes have had on the 'quality' of Portuguese democracy, as well as the country's economic and social development. In sum, the main goal of the special volume is to reflect on how far Portugal has come since 1974, in order to better understand where it is headed as we near the start of the third decade of the twenty-first century. To this end, it provides a series of original analyses of the development of Portuguese politics, sociology and economics since the transition to democracy. Drawing on research by established scholars, the volume offers an up-to-date assessment of political and economic issues that will help us to understand contemporary Portugal.

This Introduction outlines the main objectives of this special volume and provides a very brief snapshot of where Portugal stands forty-four years after the Revolution. While there are limitations to such a brief and static political and economic overview, this section of the Introduction is important in order to provide a record of where Portugal stands at the time of publication, as well as to present the economic and political context for the rest of the volume. In addition, this brief overview seeks to underscore the enormous social, political and economic progress that Portugal has made since the Revolution, and also to emphasize the challenges that the country still faces. Finally, it will also provide a starting point upon which new research on the topics addressed in this volume can be built.[1]

Objectives

This special volume examines the impact and legacy of the revolution as regards the subsequent traits and the quality of democracy in Portugal. It addresses the following questions: how did the revolution contribute to reduce political and economic inequalities? what was its role in shaping party politics and in the strengthening of accountability mechanisms? to what extent was Portuguese foreign policy shaped by this event? and are patterns of civic and political participation still conditioned by cleavages, identities and resources generated during the revolution? Moreover, this volume also analyses the impact of the Portuguese transition in other countries, and in particular its global impact in influencing other Third Wave cases of democratization.

The volume also considers the theoretical implications of the Portuguese transition, and raises questions that can be articulated by using Portugal as a case study to debate and rethink theories of revolution and democratization. Indeed, not only are revolutions rare events, but frequently they do not lead to democracy. However, Portugal represents a case of a successful and consolidated post-revolutionary democracy. Hence, the special volume examines the conditions under which revolutions originate democratic regimes and analyses whether democracies that emerge out of this pathway are different, in either quality or depth, from democracies emerging from other pathways.

---

[1] The data presented in this Introduction comes largely from the International Monetary Fund's *World Economic Outlook* database. Also, Marie-Sophie Schwarzer, et al., 'Monocle Portugal Survey', *Monocle*, 101 (March 2017), 1–62.

The examination of the Portuguese case will shed new light on the challenges (and opportunities) that countries face when undergoing such profound transformations. It draws lessons about policy and strategic options from the Portuguese experience.

Indeed, this special volume challenges the claim sometimes made that revolutionary transitions do not produce sustainable democratic regimes. Contrary to this prediction, it shows that in Portugal the 1974 revolution has resulted in democratization and resilient political stability. Indeed, democratization and European integration have promoted rather that undermined alternative domestic responses. While Europeanization, technological changes, capital market integration, and post-industrialization have affected the balance of power between governments and private actors, and have triggered new political realignments in Portugal, they have also have influenced the interests and strategies of the actors and have led to new strategies and patterns of change.

While there are already a number of books published in English that examine the Portuguese transformation over the last four decades,[2] this special volume is a significant contribution to the literature. First it examines the Portuguese political, economic and social transformation since the Revolution of 1974, and analyses the challenges that the country still faces in the second decade of the twenty-first century. Furthermore, it integrates the Portuguese modernization experience, which to date has been studied almost solely in the framework of political transitions to democracy, into the literature on European political economy. The volume also examines the consequences of the combined

---

[2] A sample of these books include: António Costa Pinto, ed., *Modern Portugal* (Palo Alto, CA: SPOSS, 1998); António Costa Pinto, ed., *Contemporary Portugal: Politics, Society and Culture* (New York: SSM, 2003); António Costa Pinto and Nuno Severiano Teixeira, eds, *Southern Europe and the Making of the European Union* (New York: SSM, 2002); Diane Ethier, *Economic Adjustment in New Democracies: Lessons from Southern Europe* (New York: St. Martin's Press, 1997); Laura Ferreira-Pereira, *Portugal in the European Union* (New York: Routledge 2014); André Freire, Marina Costa Lobo and Pedro Magalhães, *Portugal at the Polls* (New York: Lexington Books, 2002); Hugo Gill Ferreira, *Portugal's Revolution: Ten Years On* (New York: Cambridge University Press, 2011); Lawrence Graham, ed., *Contemporary Portugal: The Revolution and its Antecedents* (Austin: Texas University Press, 1979); José M. Magone, *The Changing Architecture of Iberian Politics (1974-1992): An Investigation of the Structuring of Democratic Political Systemic Culture in Semiperipheral States* (London: Edwin Mellen Press, 1995); José M. Magone, *European Portugal: The Difficult Road to Sustainable Democracy* (New York: Palgrave, 1996); José M. Magone, *Politics in Contemporary Portugal* (New York: Lynne Rienner, 2014); José M. Magone, *Iberian Trade Unionism: Democratization under the Impact of the European Union* (London: Transaction Publishers, 2001); Phil Mailer, *Portugal: The Impossible Revolution* (Oakland, CA: PM Press, 2012); Paul C. Manuel, *Uncertain Outcome* (New York: UPA, 1995); Paul C. Manuel, *The Challenges of Democratic Consolidation* (Westport, CT: Praeger, 1996); Kayman Martin, *Revolution and Counter-Revolution in Portugal* (New York: Merlin Press, 1987); Kenneth Maxwell, *The Making of Portuguese Democracy* (New York: Cambridge University Press, 1997); Daniel Nataf, *Democratization and Social Settlements* (Buffalo, NY: State University of New York Press, 1995); Sebastián Royo, *Portugal in the 21st Century* (Lanham, MD: Lexington Books, 2011); Sebastián Royo and Paul C. Manuel, eds, *Spain and Portugal in the European Union: The First Fifteen Years* (London: Frank Cass, 2003); José da Silva Lopes, ed., *Portugal and EC Membership Evaluated* (New York: St. Martin's Press, 1994); Douglas Wheeler, *Republican Portugal* (Madison: Wisconsin University Press, 1998).

processes of democratization from a multidisciplinary standpoint that includes political, economic, social, historical and sociological issues.

In addition, the volume analyses the effects of European integration in new democracies. The Portuguese experience with European integration offers one of the few instances in which integration took place in an economic, political, and institutional context markedly different from that of the other European states, and the volume explores the impact of European integration on democratic consolidation.

It also examines the sociological consequences of democratization, whose effects have been significant from a social and cultural standpoint. As part of its democratic transition, Portuguese society embarked on new processes of self-discovery. It began to come to terms with its own identity, while addressing issues such as culture, nationality, citizenship, ethnicity and politics. The revolutionary democratic transition greatly influenced these developments. At the dawn of the new millennium it would not be an exaggeration to say that the Portuguese have become 'mainstream Europeans', and that many of the cultural differences that separated the country from its European counterparts have faded as a consequence of the integration process.

At the same time, the volume ponders the legacies of the revolution for the Portuguese economy and for social policy. EU membership initially brought its own problems for the Portuguese economy. While the difficulties of the 1980s and early 1990s were successfully overcome, new challenges emerged in the new millennium. Entry to the EU has so far brought many advantages to the country, and Portugal has benefited extensively from the EU's cohesion policies, which have contributed to improving the physical infrastructure and capital stock of the country. Moreover, Portugal's trade with the EU has expanded dramatically over the last four decades, and foreign investment has flooded in. One of the main consequences of these developments has been a reduction in the economic differentials that separated the country from the European average. The culmination of this process was the (largely unexpected) participation of the country as founding participants in European Monetary Union in 1999.

Finally, the Portuguese revolutionary experience will also illustrate the economic, social, institutional and cultural challenges of this undertaking and will provide useful lessons for other countries. While the revolution and subsequent democratization have had very positive effects, they have also brought significant costs in terms of economic and social adjustment. Indeed, Portugal has suffered intense economic challenges since 2004, and has experienced serious budgetary and fiscal problems that have hampered economic growth, and led to the country's bailout in 2011.

Background: A Snapshot of Portugal in 2017

After decades of relative isolation under an authoritarian regime, the success of the democratic transition in Portugal in the second half of the 1970s paved the way for the establishment of a liberal democracy in the country. And while Portugal experienced a difficult and revolutionary democratic transition process, its overall outcome has been very positive, as we will see throughout this special volume. Indeed, since then, Portugal has experienced one of the most stable and prosperous periods in the country's modern history.

Since the transition to democracy two main parties, the centre-left Socialist Party (PS) and the centre-right Social Democratic Party (PSD), have alternated in power. Absolute majorities in parliament have been the exception, which has fostered a culture of bargaining and coalition-building. In 2009 the Socialist Party was elected for a second term on a stimulus platform, but given the depth of the crisis it was forced to introduce an austerity package immediately after the election. The adjustment programme was negotiated by the outgoing Socialist government but was left to be fully implemented by its successor, a centre-right coalition, which had won an absolute majority in the 2011 election, and, led by its Prime Minister Coelho, implemented a brutal austerity package.

In October of 2015 the country had its last general election to date. Prime Minister Pedro Passos Coelho's *Forward Portugal* coalition secured the most votes in the general election, yet it was unable to form a majority in Parliament. Portugal's President, Aníbal Cavaco Silva, charged Coelho with forming a minority government, but it was short-lived: it lasted only eleven days and collapsed, amid an intense social media campaign galvanized around the hashtag *#Thisisacoup*, when the united opposition voted against its policy programme. The Socialist Party (PS) subsequently formed a minority government with the Communist Party (PCP) and the Left Bloc (BE). As of January of 2018, this coalition is still in power.

	% of Vote	Number of Seats
People. Animals. Nature (PAN)	1.4	1
Communist Coalition (CDU)	8.3	17
Left Bloc (BE)	10.2	19
Forward Portugal Coalition	38.3	104
Socialist Party (PS)	32.4	85

TABLE 1. The Portuguese Parliament (2015–)
Source: Portuguese National Election Commission (CNE)

So far Portugal has been able to avoid the populist movements that have plagued other European countries since the start of the crisis. The combination of strong parties, like the Communist Party, which have been successful in attracting a younger generation, and the existence of new parties, like the Left Bloc, that occupy the space that left-wing parties would have held, as well as strong unions that have mobilized and articulated people's discontent, have all contributed to this development.

Portugal has a presidential system but since the transition to democracy real power has resided in the hands of the Prime Minister (PM). António Costa, leader of the Socialist Party, was elected Prime Minister after the general election of 2015. Although his party finished second in the election, he was able to put together a coalition with other leftist parties and to be voted Prime Minister. His election as PM came as a considerable surprise. Costa's Socialist Party had a long and very contentious relationship with the Communist Party since the Carnation Revolution, largely driven by ideological and personal differences, with a long history of conflict and confrontation. However, Costa was able to capitalize on the profound discontent amongst the radical left with the austerity policies of the outgoing conservative coalition government, and he was very skilful in building an unexpected leftist coalition with the Greens, the radical Left Bloc and the hard-line Communist Party, a coalition that has not only been effective in government but also has lasted far longer than most observers anticipated.

Some of the success of the coalition is rooted in Costa himself. He is a skilful political operator known for his ability to engage his opponents and unite their disparate interests. Charismatic and a good orator, he has benefitted from the backlash in Portugal against the policies of austerity that were implemented following the crisis of 2008. In this way he has been able to prove his bona fides to the markets, while gaining support at home where his popularity has increased exponentially. Polls in 2017 suggested that he was the favourite to win the next election — according to those polls the Socialists enjoyed a 5.6-point lead over the centre-right opposition.

Indeed, despite generalized scepticism and criticism, both inside and outside of Portugal, for his recklessness in entering into a 'diabolical pact' with the far left, Costa has been able to sustain his anti-austerity coalition and bring a level of stability to the country that few had believed was possible. Investors from many sectors have been impressed, and companies like Bosch, Continental, Volkswagen (which recently upgraded its Setúbal factory), Peugeot, Citroën, Embraer, Amy's Kitchen, Fujitsu, Huawei, Kagome and Microsoft have been increasing investment in the country (private investment grew by 7% in the first quarter of 2017).

Costa has also benefitted from the election of Marcelo Rebelo de Sousa as President of the Republic, in March 2016. Although the President's powers are quite limited under the Portuguese constitution, he/she has the power to dissolve parliament and call a snap election. Despite the fact that Rebelo de Sousa comes from the leading opposition party (the conservative Social Democratic

Party–PSD), he has a strong independent streak and few political attachments when it comes to making decisions. He has very extensive experience as leader of the PSD, as a member of parliament and a minister, and in the years prior to the election he gained enormous popularity and support as a journalist, with an influential Sunday TV show. While running for President he stood as an independent appealing for moderation and cross-party consensus, promising to repair political divisions and the hardship of Portugal's 2011–14 economic bailout. Although he had never previously held a top state position, he is well versed in playing to the crowd and has taken unprecedented and symbolic steps (like his tendency to eschew some of the demands of security, and his regular breaks with protocol) that have endeared him to the Portuguese people. Rebelo de Sousa's pragmatism and willingness to work with PM António Costa have contributed to the political stability of the country.

The country has emerged from the great recession in a much stronger position, and the atmosphere is upbeat. It has capitalized on increasing competitiveness by keeping its traditional trades (shoe-making, fashion, and cork production) growing, while pushing into new areas such as technology, energy and mobility.[3] Costa's soft approach to austerity has paid off politically and it has contributed to moderate growth. Yet Portugal is still vulnerable and the country still faces major risks, particularly regarding its banking sector. It is also important to note that the country has benefitted from favourable external factors, including low oil prices, looser monetary policies from the European Central bank, and a tourist boom. It also profited from the reforms implemented by the Passos Coelho's government during the bailout years.

In October 2017 the ruling Socialist Party reaped the rewards of a growing economy and won a decisive victory in local elections. They won 160 mayors (out of a total of 308 municipalities), 10 more than in 2013, and more than 38% of the votes. This was the PS's strongest electoral result in a local election in four decades of democracy, and it validated the party's strategy to turn the page on austerity. In December 2017, Mário Centeno, Portugal's Minister of Finance, was elected President of the Eurogroup of Finance Ministers, the first from a southern member state, and the first to represent a former bailout economy. It has also been interpreted as a recognition of the success of the Portuguese government's economic policies.

Economy

Portugal's economic performance in the 1990s was remarkable. Between 1994 and 2000 real GDP growth, export-led but also boosted by private consumption and fixed investment, averaged more than 3% annually and economic expansion continued for seven years. In 1996, the fifth year of expansion, GDP growth

---

[3] Portugal is playing an important role in shaping how societies might move around in urban centres in the future, and in 2018 is hosting the *Mobi Summit*, which will bring the world's leading experts to Lisbon to discuss transport trends and debate the future of mobility.

reached almost 4%, and in 2000 it was still 3.25%. The unemployment rate also fell, reaching a record low of around 4% in 2000 (one of the lowest in Europe), and inflation was brought down to just over 2% in 1999. Following the consolidation efforts prior to 1997, Portugal was also able to meet the Maastricht fiscal deficit criteria for European Monetary Union membership, by bringing the deficit down to 2.5% of GDP. One of the most important factors that contributed to this performance was the transformation of the financial sector, largely spurred by EU directives on interest rate deregulation, liberalization of the regulatory framework, privatization, and freeing of international capital movements. The privatization programme, one of the most ambitious in Europe at the time (more than 100 firms were sold), was also a contributing factor because it increased competition and enhanced productivity gains, and generated revenues that averaged more than 2% of GDP per year.

However, this performance deteriorated after 1998. The absence of stability and consensus among the leading political parties on macroeconomic policy, poor performance in educational attainment, a lack of fiscal consolidation, and the erosion of comparative advantage brought about by the accession countries from Eastern Europe, all contributed to the deterioration of Portugal's economic performance following the country's accession to the EMU.

When the global financial crisis hit Portugal, starting in the winter of 2008, the country was just coming out of a recent recession and it was still struggling with its fiscal problems. The intensity of the global crisis has been such that it has had devastating consequences for the country and it has brought to the fore the imbalances and shortcomings of its economy. Indeed, by the time the global crisis hit hardest, in 2009, the country was already encumbered with high debt (83.01% of GDP) and deficit (9.05%), weak competitiveness, high unemployment (10.63%), stagnant growth in the economy (it contracted by 2.5%), and low savings rates (7.5% of GDP). While Portugal had avoided the collapse in the property market that Ireland or Spain faced, the country was still suffering from the poor management of public finances. For instance, public sector employees were virtually guaranteed a job for life regardless of performance, which made it hard for young people to find jobs in the public sector or gain promotion.

The crisis led to a 78 billion euro bailout programme from the EU and the IMF that lasted from 2011 to 2014. The bailout's Memorandum of Understanding (MoU) imposed harsh conditions that forced the Social Democratic government coalition to adopt both fiscal consolidation and deep and painful structural reforms. It launched the country into a profound recession with higher unemployment (youth unemployment reached 37.7% in 2012), more poverty and substantial cuts to old age pensions, public salaries and the national health service. As in many other European countries, the PSD government that implemented austerity was ousted from government following the 2015 election, despite winning the election with a relative majority.

Since coming to power in 2015, Costa's PS government has implemented policies that seek to secure growth, fiscal consolidation and social cohesion. It has capitalized on the parliamentary support from the Left Bloc, the Greens and the Communist Party, moving swiftly to roll back austerity measures introduced during the bailout. At the same time, however, it has sustained its commitment to meeting fiscal targets.

Costa's government has outperformed initial forecasts, passing two budgets that were approved by Brussels and avoiding the threat of sanctions for running excessive fiscal deficits. It has become the poster child for a leftist alternative to austerity, showing that it is possible and that it can deliver both in economic growth and fiscal consolidation. GDP growth reached 1.4% by 2016 and accelerated in the final quarter, reaching 2%. The 2016 deficit fell below the threshold of 3% of GDP set by the European Monetary Union's Growth and Stability Pact (it was very close to 2%), down from 4.4% in 2015, and the lowest since the transition to democracy. Unemployment has also fallen from 12.6% to around 10%. Portugal is expected to reach a budget surplus (excluding interest payments) of about 2.5% of GDP, the highest in the EU after Greece.

Costa has successfully balanced meeting the fiscal targets imposed by the EU, by freezing consumption in areas such as health and public investment, with measures to mitigate the harsh effects of austerity from the previous government, such as restoring public sector wages, working hours, holidays and state pensions to pre-bailout levels. His 2016 budget included provisions to raise pensions, lift public sector pay, increase child benefits and social payments to low-income families, as well reduce income tax and increase support for the poor. Remarkably, the Portuguese economy has been expanding for thirteen consecutive quarters.

Despite recent economic successes, the situation (as of January 2018) is still fragile. Economic recovery has been driven largely by consumption. Many in Portugal still believe that there will be another debt crisis; and international creditors, rating agencies and financial markets are still sceptical. The combination of modest economic growth (expected to reach 1.7% in 2017), with the huge level of debt (a little under 130% of GDP) and the fragility of the banking sector, which is plagued by low profitability, have left the country vulnerable, and has been pushing up borrowing costs for the government (yields in 10-year government debt reached almost 4% at the end of 2016). Fitch Ratings, Moody's, and Standard & Poor's still rate Portugal at junk status, and the government has been complaining vigorously about it, demanding that they recognize that Portugal today is different from 2012. Today more of the Portuguese budget is spent on the payment of interest than in any other EU country and the country is still stuck in a vicious circle of low growth and structural problems. The IMF declared in 2017 that the country's recovery was losing momentum and 'running out of steam'. Any external shock could potentially have a grave negative impact on Portugal. Clearly the country is not out of the woods yet.

Banking

Portugal's eight biggest banks raised more than 26 billion euros in capital between 2008 and 2014, including state aid. The most visible problem was the bailout and the rescue of the Banco Espírito Santo, now Novo Banco. Portugal is in a group of six European countries with a non-performing loan ratio above 10%. A number of banks have had difficulties since 2016: Portugal was forced to set aside 1.8 billion euros for Banif, while the Banco Comercial Português still has to repay 750 million euros in contingent convertible bonds to the government and the Caixa Geral de Depósitos has to repay 900 million euros. Concerns over capitalization are still an issue. There is a risk that Portuguese banks will need more capital and they may have difficulties raising it in the markets, given the uncertainty regarding the restructuring of Novo Banco and the general sentiment about banks in Europe.

The banking situation in Portugal is akin to what is happening in Italy. Both are countries with economic problems and low growth that did not have a serious banking crisis during the financial crisis. However, they did not sufficiently address the problems with bad loans, which are now coming to the surface. In Portugal the crisis was detonated by the implosion of the Espírito Santo group. What is remarkable is that it happened at the time when the Troika was actively overseeing the economy of the country. And they missed it. It shows the limitations of an externally based enforcement model. They are now trying to clean up the mess.

In Portugal, unlike Spain, the bad loans are not in the construction sector (they did not have a bubble as Spain did), but instead largely in the business sector. The Banco Espírito Santo was loaded with bad loans from its own group, and the largest financial institution, the publicly owned Caixa Geral, is also loaded with bad loans from the business sector, a sector that had been doing poorly because of the economic crisis.

Another factor that is complicating matters further is the role of Spanish banks, seen by many in Portugal as taking an unduly dominant position. In December 2015 Santander purchased Banif, and over the following year there was strong speculation that the European Central Bank wanted it to buy Novo Banco as well. The latter was finally sold recently, after two years, to Lone Star, but the prospect of a Santander purchase was very controversial in Portugal. The Spanish CaixaBank has 44% of BPI (it bought Barclays' share). And other banks have left the country (Barclays and BBVA in 2015). Overall, it is a very complex and murky picture that is all aggravated by the global banking crisis, and concerns about the economic policies of the leftist government.

The Environment

Portugal suffers from acute environmental problems which have grown steadily worse since the Revolution. Some people might say that they are more important than many of the other problems facing the country. One of the most tragic manifestations of these environmental problems has been the fires that have ravaged the country for the last couple of decades. Just in October of 2017, 43 people died in more than 500 fires throughout the country, and four months previously 64 people died in fires in Pedrógão Grande. Portugal usually has the tragic distinction of leading the European Union (EU) in both the number of fires, and also in land burnt and destroyed. There have been years in which more than half of the land surface burnt and destroyed in the EU is in Portugal, despite the fact that the country only occupies 92,000 square kilometres of the 4.4 million of the EU. The reasons are varied: from the lack of stability in policies and leaderships to address the problem, to the promiscuity of trees and houses in rural areas, to the insufficient resources to fight these fires (for instance, the country has only 2000 professional firemen and relies largely on volunteers, who are often inadequately trained) and funding (the country spends 100 million euros p.a. on preventing and putting out fires, while Spain spends 2 billion euros), and the focus on fighting fires, rather than preventing them. Finally, Portugal is notable in that 85% of the country's woods are in private hands, according to the National Forest Inventory (for comparison, the figure is 75% in France, 70% in Spain and 66% in Italy), and the country lacks a reliable registry of houses, owners, or occupants. Following the disaster of Pedrógão Grande the government is working to develop a national forest registry.[4]

Energy

Portugal is harnessing its natural resources to produce clean energy. In 2016, Portugal's electricity generation came almost entirely from renewable sources (95.5%, up from 16% in 2005) and the goal is to become 100% renewable by reducing energy consumption and further developing renewables. In 2016 Portugal broke the record for the most number of hours running continuously on 100 percent renewable electricity energy sources. Fossil fuels are still the source of 38.3% of the energy produced, but the trend is downwards. Portugal has very limited indigenous oil production and is almost entirely dependent on imports. It has a well diversified supply of crude oil sources: by country, Angola was the largest oil supplier (23% of total crude oil imports), followed by Brazil, Kazakhstan, Algeria and Saudi Arabia. Demand for the cheaper natural gas, which was only introduced in the past decade, has steadily increased.

Portugal is ranked number four in worldwide wind power, with 10 GW of

---

[4] See '¿Por qué los incendios en Portugal son tan letales?' [Why are fires so lethal in Portugal?], *El País*, 20 October 2017.

installed capacity, and EDP (Energias de Portugal, formerly Electricidade de Portugal) is playing a central role in the country's energy transition. They are investing in projects such as WindFloat, an offshore wind farm that is the first floating wind-turbine platform in the world to be placed in deep ocean water. EDP has also invested in a new energy distribution grid that uses private solar panels and small wind turbines to replace the traditional distribution system, the InovCity concept that allows consumers to use smart meters, to make the country more sustainable and efficient.

Investment/External Relations

From an external standpoint Portugal views itself (in the words of its President) 'as a platform between cultures, civilizations and seas'. Small (10.6 million people) but cosmopolitan. Portuguese people are good at learning languages, and adapting to and living in different societies. Support for the European Union in Portugal runs deep, yet they also have a very strong relationship with the UK — their oldest ally. There is a historical wariness towards Spain, the big neighbour, marked by the popular saying: 'from Spain neither good winds, nor good marriages'. The country has a long history of colonialism, as well as strong relations with many of its former colonies (with which it has a strong Lusophone relationship), and still seeks to build bridges with Africa, Latin America and Asia. Portugal capitalizes effectively on its relations with its former colonies — Macau, for example, has been instrumental in fostering Chinese investments in the country, including in the banking sector.

Portugal is leaving behind its traditional inferiority complex. Sporting achievements (like the 2016 victory in the Euro championship against France), and cultural ones (like the recent win in the popular Eurovision Song Contest), or the election of former PM António Guterres as the new Secretary General of the United Nations, have elevated people's morale following the devastating crisis, and given the country a sense of collective triumph after many bitter disappointments. But more importantly, a new generation of young people are taking pride in all things Portuguese, as noted by the powerful emergence of new brands that emphasize 'Made in Portugal'. A journey through Portugal shows a country with a thriving business environment led by innovation and small business, and by its renewed enthusiasm for trade-exports, which soared from 31.5% of GDP in 2010 to 44% in 2016. Agriculture (cork, tomatoes, wood pulp, wine and olive oil) has been one of the booming sectors, with exports growing at a rate of 3–5% a year. At the same time, it is important to highlight the emergence of technology and innovation. The country is trying to make good its dream to become 'The West Coast of Europe', and the recent Web Summit (Europe's biggest technology marketplace) which took place in Lisbon in November 2016 showcases a new generation of technology companies. The country's investment in education is finally paying off.

Indeed, Portugal can be an attractive investment partner. Investors can benefit from the country's geographical location, by being the closest European country to the Americas, and near to Africa; its established infrastructure; its skilled and multilingual labour force (80% of the country's university students speak two or more languages); and the competitive incentives that are offered to attract investors, which include tax credits and a 10 billion euro fund to support innovation, research and development, and job creation.

In sum, while it is undeniable that the challenges facing the country are still daunting, Portugal is once again moving in the right direction. Prior to the 2007 crisis, EU and EMU membership was all about the benefits. Now the terms are unquestionably different, as Portugal has to face the pain of life in Euroland and adjust to this new reality. The Socialist government has been building an alternative path forward for a third way, one that moves away from the policies of austerity and seeks to balance them with policies that seek growth, equity and macroeconomic stability. While challenges remain, there has been significant progress and hence there are strong reasons for optimism.

The Special Volume

The extensive academic work on 25 April 1974 has yet to generate full agreement about the most appropriate way to understand either the events surrounding the demise of the *Estado Novo* over forty years ago or their lasting impact. This volume seeks to contribute to this debate with six articles by leading Portuguese and American social scientists. The legacies of the 1974 Carnation Revolution are the connecting link that brings all the contributions together.

The first contribution, from **Robert M. Fishman**, seeks to address two interrelated questions: first, how to conceptualize the abrupt demise of the *Estado Novo* in 1974; and second to assess the extent to which the events of that April shaped subsequent historical developments in Portugal and in the world at large. He argues that the very broad impact of the 1974 Carnation Revolution was linked to its multiple meanings and its multifaceted character, which were substantially broader than was the case for most of the regime transitions that followed during the Third Wave. According to Fishman, Portugal's transformation involved much more than the fundamental political change from authoritarian dictatorship to democracy.

António Costa Pinto analyses the role that the democratic transition in the 1970s played in the development of the Portuguese Constitution, which includes provisions that positioned it to the left of the Third Wave of democratization. This outcome is particularly perplexing because it took place under an elected Constitutional Assembly that was dominated by the moderate right and left, with a Communist minority. According to Costa Pinto this outcome had enduring consequences because the most committed defenders of the constitution were those who lost the political struggle during the most radical phase of Portuguese democratization, especially the Communists.

Camila Rodrigues and Tiago Fernandes analyse the development of the housing cooperative movement in democratic Portugal. The revolutionary period of 1974–75 led to a period of growth of neighbourhood movements in a context were the state was fragile and the hierarchical structure of society was in a process of redefinition. This led to a period of intense neighbourhood mobilization that originated either spontaneously or with the impulse of the Movement of the Armed Forces (MFA), with the objective of increasing the level of citizens' participation in the management of their own neighbourhoods. However, this development was short-lived. Indeed, Rodrigues and Fernandes show that in contemporary Portugal, and contrary to their aims during the revolution, housing cooperatives have been hindered in their capacity to act and develop a stronger policy role. They claim that successive economic policies of Portuguese governments after 1976 and the demands of European integration have gradually eroded the legacy of the 1974 revolution.

Nuno Severiano Teixeira and Reinaldo Saraiva Hermenegildo focus on the external dimension of Portugal and study the Portuguese presidencies of the European Union. Portugal has held the Presidency of the Council on three separate occasions, in 1992, 2000 and 2007. These terms correspond to different phases in Portugal's European integration process and different Portuguese positions with respect to European integration. Teixeira and Hermenegildo analyse these presidencies on three different levels, looking at the definition of their political programmes and priorities, at the organization of the diplomatic machinery and the management of various dossiers, and by making an assessment of the results obtained, from the perspective of Portuguese foreign policy and in terms of its impact on the European process. They argue that in the case of a small- or medium-sized power such as Portugal, the presidential term has even greater relevance than usual because the presidency represents a unique opportunity to influence, if not to lead, the European agenda; and also, because at certain moments in negotiations a small power might more easily achieve agreement and consensus among the great powers.

Sebastián Royo's contribution builds on his previous work on this subject and analyses how Portugal's revolutionary legacies have affected the country's economic performance in the years prior to the global financial crisis, from 1999 to 2007. His main argument is that the distinctiveness of the country's pathway from dictatorship to democracy, coupled with other crucial features of its recent political past, helped to set the stage for the subsequent economic challenges that the country experienced following accession to European Monetary Union in 1999. Royo claims that Portugal's historic path-dependency, marked by the country's distinctive democratization and its semi-peripheral economy, are still shaping the country's democracy and economic performance. The decades that followed the democratic transition have not yet fully addressed the historical challenges of a weak economy, and a weak state and civil society. Distorted governance still persists, with detrimental effects on economic performance.

The impact of both came to the fore during the recent global financial crisis and led to the country's bailout.

Finally, **Miguel Glatzer**'s article looks at the effects of the crisis, and policy responses to it, on unemployment, poverty, inequality and emigration, and analyses the Troika's effects on labour market policy in Portugal. A central theme of Glatzer's contribution is the changing nature of labour market governance in Portugal, namely from large levels of national autonomy prior to the crisis, to external imposition under bailout conditionality, to a limited rollback of some measures under the António Costa government. His article also covers related elements of pension policy, the minimum wage and anti-poverty programmes; and examines the recent rollback of some of the austerity measures imposed by the Troika.

What 25 April Was and Why It Mattered

Robert M. Fishman

Universidad Carlos III, Madrid

What exactly was 25 April an example of — or to put the matter slightly differently, how should we conceptualize the abrupt demise of the *Estado Novo* on that date in 1974 — and how did the events of that April shape subsequent historical developments in Portugal and in the world at large? Despite the existence of international scholarly consensus over the proposition that Portugal's 'Liberation by Golpe'[1] on 25 April 1974 inaugurated what would soon prove to be a worldwide wave of democratization, and the widespread agreement within contemporary Portugal over the fundamental contribution of the Carnation Revolution to the country's successful path to full democratic freedoms, many questions about the events of April 1974 — and their enduring significance — have yet to elicit full intellectual 'closure'. The large corpus of academic work on 25 April and, within Portugal, the massive socio-political commitment to telling the story of April — most prominently in the large-scale annual programme of commemoration — have yet to generate full agreement about the most appropriate way to understand the events surrounding the demise of the *Estado Novo* over forty years ago and their lasting impact.

In similar fashion, the international scholarly literature on the worldwide wave of democratization that began with Portugal lacks a shared explanation of exactly *how* the Portuguese revolution helped to make possible the global upsurge of political freedoms which had seemed unlikely prior to that date. Indeed, the absence of such an explanation in the literature can be seen to raise the question of whether Portugal's status as the first case chronologically of the global wave really is reflective of a genuinely *causal* contribution to worldwide democratization. To take up but one recent example, Kurt Weyland's influential analysis of cross-border diffusion in the Third Wave of democratization argues that the international effects of Portugal's pathway to democracy were actually quite limited.[2] Other studies of worldwide democratization

---

[1] Philippe C. Schmitter, 'Liberation by Golpe: Retrospective Thoughts on the Demise of Authoritarian Rule in Portugal', *Armed Forces and Society*, 2.1 (1975), 5–33. In this article Schmitter coined this memorable term for conceptualizing 25 April and the country's deliverance from dictatorship through a revolutionary coup on that date.

[2] Kurt Weyland, *Making Waves: Democratic Contention in Europe and Latin America since the Revolutions of 1848* (New York: Cambridge University Press, 2014).

take considerable note of Portugal's status as the chronological initiator of the global wave but fail to explain *how* the country's road to democracy may have changed circumstances and the prospects for democracy elsewhere.[3] I argue that the Carnation Revolution did in fact exert an extraordinarily broad causal impact that was linked to its multiple meanings and its multifaceted character, which was substantially broader in expanse than was the case for most of the regime transitions that followed during the Third Wave. Portugal's transformation involved much more than the fundamental political change from authoritarian dictatorship to democracy.[4] This claim is not intended to deny the extraordinary importance of political democratization in and of itself. Democracies are fundamentally different from non-democratic regimes not only in the character of political rule itself but also in a wide range of social outcomes that tend to be markedly more positive in free and representative political systems than in anti-democratic ones.[5] Some such effects may take time to manifest themselves; Huber and Stephens find that democracy tends to reduce inequality but that there is a considerable time-lag in the emergence of this outcome after a country has democratized.[6] The effects of democracy are attributable not only to policies adopted by freely chosen representatives of a country's electorate but also to the development of partially related institutions — for example in the labour relations arena[7] — and the implications of democracy for a country's insertion into the international system, as in the case of the European Union.[8] Yet having said all of this, it must be emphasized that Portugal's post-25 April road to democracy was a historically very unusual one, with much greater consequences for society, the economy and culture than more common pathways to democracy, focused more exclusively on the transformation of political rule itself.

---

[3] Guillermo O'Donnell, Philippe Schmitter and Laurence Whitehead, eds, *Transitions from Authoritarian Rule: Prospects for Democracy* (Baltimore, MD: Johns Hopkins University Press, 1986), and Samuel P. Huntington, *The Third Wave: Democratization in the Late Twentieth Century* (Norman: University of Oklahoma Press, 1991).
[4] The *Estado Novo* fits Juan Linz's classic formulation of authoritarian regimes as systems characterized by limited and non-responsive internal pluralism coupled with repression and efforts to depoliticize the population. See Juan Linz, 'Totalitarian and Authoritarian Regimes', in *Handbook of Political Science*, vol. III: *Macropolitical Theory*, ed. by Fred I. Greenstein and Nelson W. Polsby (Reading, MA: Addison-Wesley, 1975), pp. 175–411. For an important analysis of the most reformist tendency within the Portuguese authoritarian regime, and its inability to achieve its objectives in that repressive context, see Tiago Fernandes, *Nem ditadura nem revolução: a Ala Liberal e o Marcelismo (1968–1974)* (Lisbon: Dom Quixote, 2006).
[5] Adam Przeworski et al., *Democracy and Development: Political Institutions and Well-Being in the World, 1950–1990* (New York: Cambridge University Press, 2000).
[6] Evelyne Huber and John Stephens, *Democracy and the Left: Social Policy and Inequality in Latin America* (Chicago, IL: University of Chicago Press, 2012).
[7] See Sebastián Royo, 'A New Century of Corporatism?' *Corporatism in Southern Europe: Spain and Portugal in Comparative Perspective* (Westport, CT: Praeger, 2002) and Alan Stoleroff, 'Relações industriais e sindicalismo em Portugal', *Sociologia: Problemas e Práticas*, 4 (1988), 147–64.
[8] Sebastián Royo and Paul Manuel, *Spain and Portugal in the European Union: The First Fifteen Years* (London: Frank Cass, 2003).

The multiple meanings and interpretations of 25 April have been constantly evident in the collective memory of the revolution, as the recent analysis of Carvalho and Ramos Pinto underscores.[9] This multiplicity of possible meanings has led some commemorative endeavours to focus as heavily on the use of photographs and symbols as on the words intended to capture precisely the significance of what happened and what was accomplished in 1974.[10] In the international scholarly community many have seen the Portuguese pathway to democracy as a problematic one that was not only unusual but also — in their view — laden with features to be avoided if possible, rather than celebrated,[11] whereas others have identified distinctive advantages of the country's road to democracy via social revolution.[12] Although a substantial majority of the Portuguese public, crossing partisan political divisions, shares in celebrating the significance of April 1974,[13] the events of that year are not seen in precisely the same way by the totality of those involved in the annual celebrations, and others continue to hold greater or lesser reservations about the Portuguese pathway to freedom initiated on the emblematic date. In this short essay I offer a conceptualization of the 1974 events that acknowledges the bases for disagreement while also identifying multiple reasons why April 1974 *should be* celebrated for its distinctiveness as the beginning of a historically unusual social revolutionary pathway to democracy.

To a large extent, existing disagreements over the enduring significance of what happened during the revolution rest on the multifaceted nature of the Portuguese April — and its aftermath — which is to say the way in which historical events wove together analytically distinct dimensions, and processes,

---

[9] Tiago Carvalho and Pedro Ramos Pinto, 'From the "unfinished revolution" to the "defence of the revolution": Framing the Transition in Austerity-era Portugal', paper presented at the CES Conference of Europeanists, 14 July 2017, Glasgow.

[10] I have done fieldwork on the commemorations in 2004, 2006, 2012, 2014 and 2016. I discuss the commemorations and their crucial place in the country's democratic practice in Robert M. Fishman, 'Democratic Practice after the Revolution: The Case of Portugal and Beyond', *Politics & Society*, 39.2 (2011), 233–67.

[11] To a greater or lesser extent many political scientists have held such a view of the Portuguese transition. For an interpretation that elaborates this perspective see Paul Manuel, *Uncertain Outcome: The Politics of the Portuguese Transition to Democracy* (Lanham, MD: University Press of America, 1995). The best overall history of the events in English continues to be Kenneth Maxwell, *The Making of Portuguese Democracy* (Cambridge: Cambridge University Press, 1995). See also the important conceptual treatment in comparative perspective in Juan Linz and Alfred Stepan, *Problems of Democratic Transition and Consolidation: Southern Europe, South America and Post-Communist Europe* (Baltimore, MD: Johns Hopkins University Press, 1996).

[12] Robert M. Fishman, 'Rethinking the Iberian Transformations: How Democratization Scenarios Shaped Labor Market Outcomes', *Studies in Comparative International Development*, 45.3 (2010), 281–310; Robert M. Fishman and Omar Lizardo, 'How Macro-Historical Change Shapes Cultural Taste: Legacies of Democratization in Spain and Portugal', *American Sociological Review*, 78.2 (2013), 213–39; Tiago Fernandes, 'Rethinking Pathways to Democracy: Civil Society in Portugal and Spain, 1960s-2000s', *Democratization*, 22.6 (2015) 1074–1104.

[13] Marina Costa Lobo, António Costa Pinto and Pedro Magalhães, 'Portuguese Democratisation Forty Years On: Its Meaning and Enduring Legacies', *South European Society and Politics*, 21.2 (2016), 163–80.

of change. It is useful to make explicit an important methodological point: although in a certain sense historical reality and process constitute a unified whole, from an analytical standpoint it is often fruitful — or even necessary — to distinguish between different components of historical experience.[14] Both the values of socio-political actors and the theoretical perspectives of scholars can lead them to evaluate distinct analytical components of the historical whole differentially. The political, social and socialist components of the Portuguese Revolution are, in this sense, analytically distinct phenomena; differentiating between them can facilitate our consideration of April's legacies even though historically they were interwoven with one another in the lived circumstances of 1974 and 1975. I turn now to a discussion of the historical interconnections among these distinct dimensions of what occurred over forty years ago and of the legacies of these dimensions.

From its inception, the captains' coup of 25 April was an episode of political revolution that successfully inaugurated a process of democratic transition, yet at the same time the uprising of 'April's Captains' also initiated a social revolution that would soon take a turn toward a socialist transformation of the economy. The historical import of Portugal's 25 April encompasses all of these components: political revolution, democratic transition, social revolution and socialist transformation. Over four decades later, however, political forces and scholars obviously differ in the degree to which they are comfortable embracing this entire package of historical elements of the 25 April 'story'. Right-of-centre supporters of democracy can easily celebrate the toppling of the *Estado Novo* and the pathway to democratic elections initiated by April, but can hardly be expected to see the Revolution's socialist turn in as positive a light as political forces located to their left. Clearly, the left also feels a greater affinity than the right or centre-right for the Revolution's social dimensions but that is not to say that Portugal's social revolutionary pathway to democracy has been exclusively appropriated by the left. Indeed, I argue that the socio-cultural legacies of the revolution's social character exert a broadly enduring impact in Portugal today, one that in important respects encompasses political actors to the right of centre.

At the time of this writing, the lack of a full consensus over the most important elements of the Revolution's enduring legacies might appear to suggest that only those elements that elicit broad agreement genuinely held lasting importance, but in what follows I argue something quite different. I suggest that within Portugal itself the most persistent significance of the

---

[14] The distinction between analytical approaches on the one hand and the complex nature of underlying empirical reality on the other hand is a classically Weberian one. See Max Weber '"Objectivity" in Social Science and Social Policy', in Max Weber, *The Methodology of the Social Sciences* (Glencoe, IL: The Free Press, 1949), pp. 49–112. See also Robert M. Fishman, 'On Being a Weberian (after Spain's 11–14 March): Notes on the Continuing Relevance of the Methodological Perspective Proposed by Weber', in *Max Weber's 'Objectivity' Reconsidered*, ed. by Laurence McFalls (Toronto: University of Toronto Press, 2007), pp. 261–89.

country's quite distinctive pathway to democracy is to be found, in various ways, in the *cultural legacies* of social revolution and their ongoing impact on socio-political life; that is, the basic understandings of democracy and forms of conduct by social and political actors are strongly conditioned by the country's pathway to democracy. Additionally, and counter to many existing assumptions, I argue that the reason why 25 April helped to unlock the global potential for widespread democratization was linked to the Revolution's specifically *socialist* turn and the fact that in the years following 1974 Portugal built a new system that was simultaneously committed to the construction of a (partially) socialist economy and a liberal representative democracy that guarantees all of the essential freedoms found in other full democracies. The explicitly socialist commitments of the new system, initially enshrined in the Constitution written by the Assembly elected on 25 April 1975, just one year after the Carnation Revolution, were ultimately reversed by the Constitutional revision of 1989 permitting the reprivatization of businesses affected by the large-scale nationalizations that took place during the revolutionary period.[15] Nonetheless, for important reasons the country's institutionalized effort to simultaneously construct socialism and representative democracy held major international relevance, especially during the historically crucial early years of the Third Wave. I develop the basis for this claim below and in a separate discussion elsewhere.[16] In the analysis that follows I turn to the factors and dynamics that explain how and why a political revolution quickly assumed first a broadly social character and then an explicitly socialist one.

The *Estado Novo*'s effort to maintain the country's colonial possessions in Africa, despite the growth of major armed insurgencies pressing for the independence of these territories, stands as an obvious underlying cause of the broadly social turn taken by the Portuguese Revolution that began in April 1974. Indeed, the colonial wars created major strains within the Armed Forces and served to condition virtually all aspects of the revolutionary transition, as Nancy Bermeo has argued.[17] In this respect and in others, the Portuguese case fits remarkably well Theda Skocpol's theoretical model of conditions favourable to social revolution.[18] Moreover, the existence under the *Estado Novo* of well-organized sources of socio-political resistance, such as the Portuguese Communist Party and other oppositional movements and parties, also closely fits the Skocpolian model of conditions ultimately conducive to

---

[15] On the privatizations see, María Asensio Menchero, *El proceso de la reforma del sector público en el sur de Europa: estudio comparativo de España y Portugal* (Madrid: Instituto Juan March, 2001), and Fernando Freire de Sousa and Ricardo Cruz, *O processo de privatizações em Portugal* (Porto: Associação Industrial Portuense, 1995).
[16] Robert M. Fishman, 'What Made the Third Wave Possible? Historical Contingency and Meta-Politics in the Genesis of Worldwide Democratization', forthcoming in *Comparative Politics*, 50.4 (July 2018).
[17] Nancy Bermeo, 'War and Democratization: Lessons from the Portuguese Experience', *Democratization*, 14.3 (2007), 388–406.
[18] Theda Skocpol, *States and Social Revolution* (New York: Cambridge University Press, 1979).

social revolution. However, more proximate factors also deserve mention. The hierarchical status of the leading actors in the 25 April uprising — namely, as captains whose collective initiative directly challenged the military's internal hierarchy and discipline — coupled with the rapid internal politicization of the Armed Forces following 25 April, contributed to the swift emergence of a state crisis — which is to say the erosion of the state's capacity to use force to guarantee any given conception of legality. State crisis effectively differentiated the Portuguese transition to democracy from other early Third Wave instances of democratization,[19] and — as many excellent analyses of the social revolution have established[20] — the direction taken by social mobilizations during the revolution was powerfully shaped by this factor.

However, despite the considerable causal significance of state crisis, an equally important conditioning factor was the strong upsurge and the political involvements of civil society from 25 April onward.[21] Indeed the events of 25 April were strongly marked by the intermingling of the rebellious military with civilian supporters who rapidly filled the streets of Lisbon. What began as a military coup led primarily by hierarchical intermediaries had become much more than that by the end of that day and, once the toppling of the old order gave way to the construction of new arrangements, the role of social mobilization grew in importance. Both the defeat of the *Estado Novo* and the articulation of new demands and understandings involved social pressures from below, alongside the decisive role of the Armed Forces Movement that brought tanks onto the streets of Lisbon. Crucially, the partial inversion of hierarchies that began inside the rebellious military units that marched on Lisbon spread quickly to institutions of both state and society — initially in the form of the purges analysed by António Costa Pinto,[22] and later in multiple forms of social mobilization and change inside neighbourhoods, schools, enterprises and other social institutions. It is crucially important to underscore the fact that

---

[19] Robert M. Fishman, 'Rethinking State and Regime: Southern Europe's Transition to Democracy', *World Politics*, 42 (1990), 422–40.

[20] See Nancy Bermeo, *The Revolution within the Revolution* (Princeton, NJ: Princeton University Press, 1986); John Hammond, *Workers and Neighborhood Movements in the Portuguese Revolution* (New York: Monthly Review Press, 1988), Rafael Duran Muñoz, *Contención y transgresión: las movilizaciones sociales y el estado en las transiciones española y portuguesa* (Madrid: Centro de Estudios Políticos y Constitucionales, 2000); Diego Palacios Cerezales, *O Poder caiu na rua* (Lisbon: Imprensa de Ciências Sociais, 2003); and most recently Pedro Ramos Pinto, *Lisbon Rising: Urban Social Movements in the Portuguese Revolution, 1974–75* (Manchester: Manchester University Press, 2013).

[21] The transition theorists Guillermo O'Donnell and Philippe Schmitter place considerable importance on what they refer to as the upsurge of civil society in the context of regime transitions. See Guillermo O'Donnell and Philippe Schmitter, *Transitions from Authoritarian Rule: Tentative Conclusions about Uncertain Transitions* (Baltimore, MD: Johns Hopkins University Press, 1986). For an empirical discussion of civil society in the Portuguese case see Tiago Fernandes, 'Rethinking Pathways to Democracy'.

[22] António Costa Pinto, 'Settling Accounts with the Past in a Troubled Transition to Democracy: The Portuguese Case', in *The Politics of Memory: Transitional Justice in Democratizing Societies*, ed. by A. Barahona de Brito et al. (Oxford: Oxford University Press, 2001), pp. 65–91; and António Costa Pinto, 'Authoritarian Legacies, Transitional Justice and State Crisis in Portugal's Democratization', *Democratization*, 13.2 (2006), 173–204.

the social revolution was not only manifested through the challenge to existing property relations — which is to say its socialist turn. In a multiplicity of ways the revolution involved mobilization of erstwhile social subordinates and their assertion of new demands to change existing social relations in matters involving culture, residence and gender relations[23] — as well as economic production, the arena that is emphasized by interpretations that highlight the revolution's socialist project. Thus the socialist turn that the revolution soon took was preceded by its more pervasively social character. Moreover, alongside the partial inversion of hierarchies and the growing demands for changed social arrangements in multiple arenas, the revolution was marked by a broad-ranging dynamic of cultural change conditioned by this new social context.[24]

The cultural change initiated by the revolution took many forms and included elements of both bottom-up and top-down processes, just as was the case with more strictly political elements of the social revolution.[25] The revolution's emblematic cultural dynamization campaign, which attempted to transform civic and cultural sensibilities in rural and more or less traditionalist areas, was launched by the revolutionary authorities and, in that sense, can be seen as a 'top-down' initiative, but it was sustained and promoted by the bottom-up commitments and enthusiasm of those who participated.[26] Other major cultural components of the country's rapid transformation after 25 April took the form of more or less spontaneous and bottom-up endeavours such as the emergence of new symbols, types of expression and discourse. Revolutionary songs, posters and poetry, along with the rapid adoption of red carnations as a symbol of the revolution, all contributed to the speedy transformation of meanings, practices and values. Cultural change proved to be far more widespread and enduring than in the case of more conventional political transitions in other national cases. As Donatella della Porta has recently argued, the emotions generated by rapid and deep forms of systemic change help to generate the collective energy needed for this to happen, and thereby make revolutionary transitions fundamentally different from more reform-oriented ones.[27] The revolution's cultural side and energies have helped to underpin the massive effort involved in telling the story of April on an annual basis, a narrative undertaking that has in turn helped to shape ongoing forms of democratic practice in the

---

[23] On gender relations see Virgínia Ferreira, 'Engendering Portugal: Social Change, State Politics and Women's Mobilization', in *Modern Portugal*, ed. by António Costa Pinto (Palo Alto, CA: The Society for the Promotion of Science and Scholarship, 1998), pp. 162–88.
[24] Robert M. Fishman, 'Democratic Practice after the Revolution: The Case of Portugal and Beyond', *Politics & Society*, 39.2 (2011), 233–67.
[25] On the revolution's mix of bottom-up and top-down dynamics, an important recent source is Pedro Ramos Pinto, *Lisbon Rising*.
[26] Sónia Vespeira de Almeida, 'Campanhas de dinamização cultural e acção cívica do MFA: uma etnografia retrospectiva', *Arquivos da Memória*, n.s., 2 (2007), 47–65.
[27] Donatella della Porta, *Where Did the Revolution Go? Contentious Politics and the Quality of Democracy* (New York: Cambridge University Press, 2016).

country.[28] Indeed, I argue that cultural phenomena play a fundamental role in the revolution's most enduring legacies.

This emphasis on culture is not meant to undervalue or question the central role of the revolution's political essence. From day one the revolution was explicitly committed to building democracy; the promise to hold free and competitive elections was vital to the country's synthesis of democratic and social revolution. The institutional charge of the Assembly chosen by voters one year after the toppling of the *Estado Novo* in 1974 was explicitly centred on the writing of a new Constitution. Standard political actors such as political parties are part of this story, but only one component of it.[29] The guiding charter of the new democratic system was conditioned both by the verdict of voters at the polls on 25 April 1975 and the revolution which continued in the streets while the document was being crafted.[30] Moreover, whereas some revolutionary forces saw the liberal guarantees of representative democracy as an inconvenient hindrance to the promotion of socialist objectives and, as a result, favoured alternative institutional forms of political rule, the defenders of full democratic freedoms ultimately won out in all relevant terrains: at the ballot box, inside the emergent representative institutions, in the streets and in ongoing divisions inside the military as well. Portuguese political actors did everything necessary to guarantee the fully democratic character of the new system but at the same time they did much more than that, extending the country's transformation into social, cultural and economic terrains.

The fact that Portugal's revolutionary road to democracy transformed much more than simply the political system itself raises the obvious question of how the legacies of the revolution's social dimensions have shaped its lasting effects. A good deal of research offers support for the claim that the social revolution left important cultural legacies that are manifested both in certain individual-level dispositions and in various macro-societal outcomes that have been conditioned by the relatively inclusionary way in which Portuguese actors understand and practise democracy.[31] The legacies of revolution manifested in contemporary Portuguese democratic practice are found in the relative openness of institutional power holders to the voices of protest in the streets — and, as a result, the tendency for interactions between protesters and office

---

[28] Robert M. Fishman, 'Networks and Narratives in the Making of Civic Practice: Lessons from Iberia', in *Varieties of Civic Innovation: Deliberative, Collaborative, Network and Narrative Approaches*, ed. by Jennifer Girouard and Carmen Sirianni (Nashville, TN: Vanderbilt University Press), pp. 159–80.

[29] See Carlos Jalali, *Partidos e Democracia em Portugal, 1974–2005* (Lisbon: Imprensa de Ciências Sociais, 2007), and Marco Lisi, *Party Change, Recent Democracies and Portugal: Comparative Perspective* (Lanham, MD: Lexington Books, 2015).

[30] On the Constitution see Pedro C. Magalhães, 'Explaining the Constitutionalization of Social Rights: Portuguese Hypotheses and a Cross-National Test', in *The Social and Political Foundations of Constitutions*, ed. by Denis J. Galligan and Mila Versteeg (New York: Cambridge University Press, 2013), pp. 432–68; and Mónica Brito Vieira and Filipe Carreira da Silva, *O momento constituinte: os direitos sociais na Constituição* (Coimbra: Almedina, 2010).

[31] Fishman, 'Democratic Practice after the Revolution'.

holders to take the form of 'conversation'[32] — and also in the tendency for institutional actors to treat the concerns of low-income and socially marginal actors as fully legitimate. These features of democratic practice have, in turn, impacted upon many other outcomes. The macro-level outcomes in question include the country's relative success in maintaining a substantially lower level of unemployment than neighbouring Spain,[33] various outcomes in the housing arena,[34] and the distributional impact of austerity policies during the long crisis that began with the worldwide Great Recession of 2008. Indeed, the most rigorous available cross-national analysis of the distributional consequences of south European austerity policies,[35] and the most recent Eurofound data from 2017,[36] coincide in showing that inequality actually decreased slightly in Portugal during the crisis whereas it increased substantially in other south European countries such as Spain. These recent data reinforce the empirical basis for earlier arguments that the contrasting pathways to democracy of the neighbouring countries of the Iberian Peninsula put in place conditions, and ways of understanding democratic practice, that have tended to generate a growing list of divergent outcomes in the two countries.[37]

This is not to say that the effects of austerity were negligible in Portugal, but instead to note that in purely distributional terms the consequences of such policies were less harsh in Portugal than in the rest of southern Europe. On at least one crucial occasion — the reversal of government policy in September 2012 regarding the initially regressive plan to switch the collection of the Taxa Social Única (social security tax) from employers to workers — it is clear that voices of protest in the streets managed to move Portuguese austerity-era policies in a direction that was fully congruent with the research findings mentioned above. A proposed policy change that would have redistributed a significant percentage of the country's GDP from workers to employers was withdrawn due to social pressure expressed in the streets. In other southern European countries the social pressure of demonstrations in the streets was not lesser in magnitude, but the ability of such pressures from below to change government policy was much more limited. In Portugal protesters managed to keep the distributional structure of austerity policies from turning sharply regressive.[38]

---

[32] Robert M. Fishman and David W. Everson, 'Mechanisms of Social Movement Success: Conversation, Disruption and Displacement', *Revista Internacional de Sociología*, 74.4 (2016), 1–10.
[33] Fishman, 'Rethinking the Iberian Transformations'.
[34] Robert M. Fishman, 'How Civil Society Matters in Democratization: Setting the Boundaries of Post-transition Political Inclusion', *Comparative Politics*, 49.3 (2017), 391–409.
[35] Manos Matsaganis and Chrysa Leventi, 'The Distributional Impact of Austerity and the Recession in Southern Europe', *South European Society and Politics*, 19.3 (2014), 393–412.
[36] See Eurofound (2017), *Income Inequalities and Employment Patterns in Europe before and after the Great Recession*, Publications Office of the European Union, Luxembourg.
[37] Robert M. Fishman, 'Legacies of Democratizing Reform and Revolution: Portugal and Spain Compared', Working Paper 1–05 (Lisbon: Instituto de Ciências Sociais, 2005).
[38] Fishman and Everson, 'Mechanisms of Social Movement Success'.

The legacies of the revolution are also found in individual-level phenomena such as cultural tastes, an arena in which Portuguese young people have been found to have more in common with their counterparts in northern Europe than with the youth of other southern European countries, and crucially this pattern has been shown to be a clear legacy of the country's revolutionary path to democracy.[39] The type of cultural dispositions that cultural sociologists refer to as 'omnivorous', reflected for example in the simultaneous interest of some 'cultural consumers' in multiple genres of music instead of only one or two varieties, have been far more common among those Portuguese born after 25 April than among their counterparts of the same age cohort in Spain or in other southern European countries. On the other hand, older residents of the Iberian Peninsula, born prior to the 1970s transitions, are not systematically differentiated from one another by country. For example, young Portuguese musical consumers are fundamentally different from their Spanish counterparts but older Portuguese and Spanish musical consumers are virtually indistinguishable from one another in their degree of 'omnivorous' enthusiasm for multiple musical forms.[40] This finding is of considerable theoretical interest because research in cultural sociology has shown that enthusiasts of cultural diversity tend also to be more tolerant on political matters and are more commonly found in social contexts characterized by relatively high levels of education and income. The fact that this outcome is found in contemporary Portugal even though the country continues to suffer from a relatively low level of per capita GDP for western Europe underscores the magnitude of the specifically cultural transformation made possible by 25 April and its legacies in crucial institutions such as the country's school system.[41] As a legacy of the revolution, Portugal's educators came to see the school system as an arena for activating the cultural potential of students and their capacity to act autonomously.[42]

Similarly — and, as in the previous example, partly due to the impact of post-revolutionary practice in the country's educational system — Portugal has been found to perform remarkably well in certain indicators of citizenship practice.[43] A large-scale cross-national survey on forms of citizenship practice found that despite the assumptions of some scholars that Portugal is a relative civic laggard, in fact it scored first internationally in citizen involvement in the electronic public sphere. Both in the predisposition of respondents to participate in internet fora for the exchange of views and in the relative size of the public

---

[39] Robert M. Fishman and Omar Lizardo, 'How Macro-Historical Change Shapes Cultural Taste: Legacies of Democratization in Spain and Portugal', *American Sociological Review*, 78.2 (2013), 213–39.
[40] Ibid.
[41] Ibid.
[42] See Stephen Stoer, *Educação, Estado e desenvolvimento em Portugal* (Lisbon: Livros Horizonte, 1982) and Stephen Stoer, *Educação e mudança social em Portugal, 1970–1980: uma década de transição* (Porto: Afrontamento, 1986).
[43] Robert M. Fishman and Manuel Villaverde Cabral, 'Socio-Historical Foundations of Citizenship Practice: After Social Revolution in Portugal', *Theory & Society*, 45 (2016), 531–53.

audience for television news, Portugal ranked first among the twenty countries for which data was collected. In the proclivity of respondents to engage in political conversation with others in the hope of influencing their political thinking, Portugal's ranking was somewhat lower, but among young people born after 25 April the country scored relatively highly and — as in the case of the study on cultural tastes — the cultural or civic sophistication of young people was quite evident among graduates of the country's high schools.[44] Indeed, the culturally and civically enabling effects of education that manifest themselves in many countries primarily among graduates of universities are to be found in Portugal among those exposed to the high school system, a far broader sector of the population than those who complete a university degree.[45] Moreover, as noted above, this effect is limited to those born after 25 April and who can be seen as the products of the post-revolutionary educational system.

This is not to say that all of the legacies of the past are positive, or that Portugal performs well on all individual-level indicators. Clearly, political disappointment and disengagement have become quite common for a variety of reasons.[46] Significant research findings suggest that at least in some local contexts the ultimate reversal of the nationalizations that marked the socialist dimension of the revolution ended up generating civic disengagement.[47] However, on balance the positive legacies appear to vastly outweigh negative ones. The breadth and depth of these legacies is reflective, at least in part, of the fusion during the revolutionary process of bottom-up and top-down dynamics of mobilization and transformation. The basis for and the effects of the social revolution were quite extensive ones.[48]

Thus both the political and the social dimensions of the Carnation Revolution have left important long-lasting legacies in contemporary Portugal. Despite the common tendency of many citizens to emphasize the country's failures or difficulties,[49] the distinctive achievements of certain elements of the recent past are considerable ones. What of the lasting impact of the socialist direction taken by the Revolution, but ultimately reversed years later? The effort to change the capitalist nature of the economy was, after all, a major component of the overall set of endeavours pursued after 25 April. At least on the surface it would seem that the reprivatizations of 1989–90 essentially erased that chapter of the country's history; moreover, as noted above, some research findings suggest that the reversal of the revolutionary-era nationalizations

---

[44] Ibid.
[45] Ibid.
[46] See Pedro Magalhães, 'Disaffected Democrats: Political Attitudes and Political Action in Portugal', *West European Politics*, 28.5 (2005), 973–91.
[47] Michael Baum, 'Workers' Control and Changes in Political Culture: Portugal's Alentejo 20 Years after the Revolution', *South European Society and Politics*, 2.1 (1997), 1–35.
[48] Pedro Ramos Pinto, *Lisbon Rising*.
[49] See Boaventura de Sousa Santos, *Portugal: ensaio contra a autoflagelação* (Coimbra: Almedina, 2011).

may have contributed to political disengagement, at least in certain settings.[50] However, I argue that there was one extremely important positive effect of the Revolution's interweaving of socialist and democratic objectives, one that contributed greatly to the worldwide Third Wave of Democratization that began in Portugal on 25 April 1974. Many failed episodes of democratization, especially during Europe's interwar period but also more recently, were at least partially conditioned by political conflict over the nature of the economy. In numerous instances of 'democratic breakdown', the interrelations between advocates of opposing models for the economy became severely conflictual in ways that proved incompatible with democratic survival.[51]

Robert Dahl has classically argued that democracy requires 'mutual tolerance' between political adversaries,[52] but prior to Portugal's Carnation Revolution mutual tolerance between advocates of capitalism and socialism was often absent from numerous political systems in which political actors disagreed over the best way to organize economic life. Advocates of systemic economic change and proponents of the existing economic system alike were often deeply sceptical of the viability of maintaining democratic institutions in the midst of political conflict over transformation of the ownership structure of the economy. Fearing that their political opponents would not allow an effort to transform the economy as a result of a democratic electoral outcome, anti-capitalist actors in many countries had instead preferred non-electoral strategies to pursue their objectives. Many actors on the right saw pro-socialists as a threat not only to the capitalist economy but also to other elements of the existing order and came to favour more or less authoritarian responses. Both on the left and the right, the lack of mutual tolerance between advocates of socialism and capitalism had contributed to the growth of anti-democratic perspectives and conduct — a broadly transnational impediment to the global spread of democracy. I argue that this systematic impediment to successful democratization in countries where much public debate centred on the nature of economic organization was fundamentally transformed by the Portuguese case where new democratic institutions and a systematic commitment to the pursuit of socialist economic relations were simultaneous features of the post-25 April transformation of the country. The Portuguese experience showed political actors elsewhere that socialism and democracy could be simultaneously pursued with remarkable success.

Important recent research on Latin America has shown that the improved prospects for democracy following the beginning of the Third Wave were strongly linked to a change in the *mind-set* of political actors, one that increased the level of normative commitment to democracy with a corresponding shift

---

[50] See footnotes 25 and 47.
[51] Juan Linz, *The Breakdown of Democratic Regimes: Crisis, Breakdown & Reequilibration* (Baltimore, MD: Johns Hopkins University Press, 1978).
[52] Robert Dahl, *Polyarchy* (New Haven, CT: Yale University Press, 1973).

in forms of political conduct.[53] I suggest that it was precisely through this mechanism that 25 April and the Portuguese efforts to simultaneously construct socialism and democracy contributed to making possible the global spread of democracy. After failures to pursue democracy and socialism simultaneously in other national settings, the experience of Portugal showed not only that such a project could be successfully advanced but also that advocates and opponents of socialism could coexist in a democracy that guaranteed full rights to all. Shortly before Portugal's post-25 April success, the overthrow of the democratically elected socialist government of Salvador Allende in Chile and the crushing of the Prague Spring by Soviet tanks had reinforced existing doubts in many sectors about the viability of pursuing the goals of socialism and democracy simultaneously. However, electorally significant political forces — for example in France where Mitterrand's 1981 election victory was tied to the promise to promote these two goals[54] — remained committed to both principles. Without the positive lesson provided by Portugal, the prospects for democracy would have been much weaker than they quickly became in the early stages of the Third Wave. The global neoliberal era made the question of socialism at least somewhat less 'current' after the mid-1980s than prior to that date. Political efforts to transform the economy in a socialist direction are clearly much less common today than at the time of the Carnation Revolution. This suggests that the connection between political and economic systems is likely as much a matter of historical contingencies as of functionally set interrelationships. But in the specific historical setting of the 1970s, Portugal's simultaneous pursuit of democracy and socialism held broad implications that in effect inaugurated the Third Wave.

The events of 25 April 1974 — and the process of change that they initiated — did much more than simply bring to an end the anti-democratic rule of the *Estado Novo*; Portugal's pathway from dictatorship to democracy fully deserves a firmer and deeper place in our collective sense of democracy's historical advance than that occupied by more routine transitions to democracy. The Carnation Revolution led to transformations in Portuguese social relations and culture that left in place a way of understanding and practising democracy that has been deeply marked by the system's social revolutionary origins. This, in turn, has made possible a form of democratic practice that is more fully inclusionary than in otherwise similar political systems and which, as a result, places the country's representative system closer to the democratic ideal of full political equality among citizens. In Portugal's post-revolutionary democracy the principle of political equality is not limited to the ballot box but also shapes developments in the important terrains of agenda-setting and public policy-

---

[53] See Scott Mainwaring and Aníbal Pérez-Liñán, *Democracies and Dictatorships in Latin America: Emergence, Survival, and Fall* (New York: Cambridge University Press, 2013).
[54] See George Ross, Stanley Hoffmann and Sylvia Malzacher, eds, *The Mitterrand Experiment* (Cambridge: Polity Press, 1987).

making. The range of actors that matters in such cases is broader and more socially inclusive than in otherwise similar cases.[55] In this sense Portuguese democracy shows genuinely enduring marks of its beginnings in social revolution. The socialist turn of the Portuguese Revolution clearly did not hold the same lasting power. The large-scale nationalizations of the revolutionary period were later reversed and the Constitution amended to make that possible. Nonetheless I argue that the socialist component of the revolution also held an enduring significance of sorts, a truly global significance that contributed to changing the mind-set of political actors in other countries during the crucial early years of the Third Wave. Somewhat paradoxically, this enduring significance was more political than economic. The process of change that began in April 1974 showed that it was indeed politically possible to construct a new system simultaneously committed to the guarantee of full democratic liberties and the construction of a socialist economy. The failure of such efforts in earlier attempts in Chile, Czechoslovakia and other countries had — for many political actors — generated a sense that attempts to fundamentally transform the ownership structure of an economy in a democratic setting were destined to fail. The absence of what Robert Dahl classically referred to as 'mutual tolerance' between political adversaries committed to divergent economic agendas had been a strong impediment to global democratization. The events unleashed by an uprising of Portuguese captains on 25 April 1974 changed that reality — along with many others.

The broad implications of Portugal's post-25 April revolutionary pathway to democracy help to explain why the Carnation Revolution is so actively remembered and commemorated. In this regard, as in many other ways, Portugal's post-revolutionary democracy is exceptional in comparative terms. Whereas many Greeks look to the student uprising against the Colonels' junta rather than the democratic transition itself,[56] and Spaniards lack a universally shared date of democratic success evoking enthusiasm and celebration, Portugal's yearly anniversary of liberation from the dictatorship of the *Estado Novo* is energetically commemorated both within official institutions and outside them, in the streets. The annual session of parliament, the yearly demonstration in central Lisbon led by the 25 April Association, and countless other commemorative activities large and small clearly establish democratic Portugal as a country uncommonly committed to remembering, retelling and celebrating its pathway of transformation from dictatorship to democracy through a historically unusual and socially expansive process. A full understanding of what 25 April was helps to explain why — and how much — the revolution mattered. Indeed, this essay argues that how much it mattered helps to clarify what it *was*, and what it *was* helps to explain *why* it

---

[55] See Robert M. Fishman, 'How Civil Society Matters in Democratization'.
[56] Kostis Kornetis, *Children of the Dictatorship: Student Resistance, Cultural Politics, and the 'Long 1960s' in Greece* (Oxford: Berghahn Books, 2013).

mattered so much. Portugal's experience clearly suggests that where democracy is brought into existence by a social revolutionary process that is genuinely and fully democratic, this pathway of transformation tends to hold major lasting benefits. However the country's experience also clearly shows how this unusual experience was rooted in quite unusual circumstances, contingencies and conditions. Social scientists have argued that circumstances that are historically unusual can at times generate consequences that hold widespread importance and relevance, for example when distinctive conditions help to produce new forms of practice that can serve as a 'model' of widespread utility. Portugal's 25 April holds a universal significance that is even greater than suggested by its status as the initiator of the Third Wave, but April's story is one that cannot be easily replicated. Thus in the final analysis it is the distinctiveness of the Carnation Revolution, including its preconditions and consequences, that provides Portugal's unusual pathway to liberation from dictatorship with a significance that merits broad attention, not only by those who specialize in the study of the country or who are Portuguese themselves but also by a far larger 'population' of scholars and observers.

Constitution-Making and the Democratization of Portugal: An Enduring Legacy

António Costa Pinto

Instituto de Ciências Sociais, Universidade de Lisboa

Of all the liberal democracies that emerged from the so-called Third Wave of democratic transitions, Portugal's was perhaps the one that inherited a constitution most anchored to the left.[1] The Portuguese Constitution of 1976 not only declared Portugal a democracy in 'transition to socialism', it also consecrated many of the dynamics of the most troubled phase of democratization: the 'socialization of the means of production', or the agrarian reform, 'as a tool for the construction of a socialist society'.[2] During the consolidation phase, two constitutional revisions removed some of these principles, notably the irreversibility of nationalizations, but many remained, leaving Portuguese democracy with a durable legacy. In 2008, when Portugal suffered its third bailout in democratic times, appeals to the Constitution and the quite independent Constitutional Court were important elements in anti-austerity campaigns by social movements as a main element blocking the attempts of the government to challenge social rights.

Elections to the Constituent Assembly held on 25 April 1975, one year after the overthrow of the dictatorship, marked the beginning of a split between the moderate parties that won the elections and their military allies on the one hand, and other sections of the Armed Forces Movement (MFA — Movimento das Forças Armadas) supported by the Portuguese Communist Party (PCP — Partido Comunista Português) and parties of the extreme left on the other. Now armed with electoral legitimacy, the Socialist Party (PS — Partido Socialista), the centre-right Popular Democratic Party (PPD — Partido Popular Democrático) and the right-wing Social Democratic Centre (CDS — Centro Democrático Social), whose combined forces represented the majority in the Constituent

---

[1] Parts of this article were presented at the conference 'From Revolution to Disillusion: Portugal's Democracy after 40 Years', Center for European Studies, Harvard University, 14 November 2014, and 'Model Transitions? Rethinking the Success Story of Southern European Democratization', St Antony's College, Oxford, 18 May 2016. It is part of the Project HAR2015-64348-P, Dictaduras y Democracias en el Siglo XX: un estudio comparado de Grecia, Portugal y España, of the University of Zaragoza.

[2] Constituição da República Portuguesa. Texto originário da Constituição, aprovada em 2 de Abril de 1976 <https://www.parlamento.pt/parlamento/documents/crp1976.pdf>.

Assembly, led an anti-Communist political struggle that intensified during what became known as the 'Hot Summer' of 1975. It was only with the victory of the moderate officers and their allies on 25 November 1975 that the balance of power swung in the direction of a swift institutionalization of democracy.

However, as the situation was becoming more radicalized in the streets, the moderate and right-wing parties had a majority in the Constitutional Assembly. In the end the Constitution reflected these tensions and contained progressive principles that contradicted in theory the political struggle that was taking place within society. Indeed, while the PS and its centre-right allies were establishing an anti-Communist front on the streets, as well as in national and international institutions, they were also using the Constituent Assembly, in which they had an overwhelming majority, to legitimate their struggle and adopt principles that the PCP and its allies in the Portuguese Democratic Movement (MDP/CDE — Movimento Democrático Português) could support. MFA officers exercised important influence over the Constitution, although their concerns focused mainly on their institutionalization. In fact, while the future semi-presidential nature of the regime and the constitutionalization of the Council of the Revolution (CR — Conselho da Revolução) were the result of a pact agreed between parts of the military, the same cannot be said of many of the principles approved in the meantime. The aim of this article is to find elements that can explain this apparent puzzle that had an almost immediate consequence: with the consolidation of democracy, the most committed defenders of the Constitution were those who lost the political struggle during the hot summer of 1975, especially the Communists.

The article proceeds as follows. In the first part, it frames the process leading to the institutionalization of Portuguese democracy and analyses political developments right up to the calling of elections to the Constituent Assembly. It will then explain the 'parallel history' of the political radicalization during the hot summer of 1975 and the work carried out in the Constituent Assembly. Finally, it will analyse the final discussions that led to the second MFA–Political Parties pact when, after 25 November 1975, the military moved closer to the moderate political parties, leading to the swift institutionalization of democracy following the approval of the Constitution in 1976.

25 April 1974: Democratization and Decolonization

On 25 April 1974, a bloodless military coup put an end to more than four decades of dictatorship in Portugal (1926–74). Unshackled by international pro-democratizing forces and occurring during the Cold War, the coup led to a severe crisis of the state that was aggravated by the simultaneous processes of democratic transition and the decolonization of what was Europe's last colonial empire.[3]

---

[3] António Costa Pinto, *O fim do império português* (Lisbon: Livros Horizonte, 2000).

Comparative literature on democratic transitions has always incorporated the Portuguese case; however, some of its characteristics — particularly the role of the military, the crisis of the state, and the dynamics of the social movements — are difficult to integrate into the comparative analysis of democratization. As Juan Linz and Alfred Stepan noted: 'we all too often tend to see [Portugal] in the framework set by later transition processes', forgetting the greater degree of uncertainty and the extremely conflicted path of regime change that, according to some authors, 'was not a conscious transition to democracy'.[4]

The nature of the Portuguese dictatorship tells us little about the nature of the country's transition to democracy. Salazarism was close to the Linzian ideal-type of authoritarian regime: it was a regime that survived the 'fascist era', and was not too dissimilar in nature to the final phase of neighbouring Spain's Franco regime, despite its single party being weaker and its 'limited pluralism' greater.[5] The singularity of the collapse of the dictatorship resides in the military intervention by junior officers, a rare — if not unique — case in the twentieth century. The colonial war being waged by the regime on three fronts, in Angola, Mozambique and Guinea-Bissau, from 1961 onwards made the captains protagonists in the country's political transformation. In 1968, Salazar was replaced by Marcelo Caetano, who initiated a limited and timid regime 'liberalization' that was swiftly halted by the worsening Colonial War. The inability of Salazar's successor to resolve some of the dilemmas caused by the war provoked the coup d'état in April 1974. This was a 'non-hierarchical' military coup that had a political programme promoting democratization and decolonization.

The prior existence of a semi-legal and clandestine opposition to Salazarism, although disconnected from the military officers who led the coup, was of crucial importance. It constituted a political option legitimated by the struggle against dictatorship. The replacement of Salazar by Marcelo Caetano in 1968 gave rise to a two-year process of 'liberalization' that, while cut short, allowed for the consolidation of a 'liberal wing' of dissidents opposed to the dictatorship. The creation of the Society for Economic and Social Development (SEDES — Sociedade para o Desenvolvimento Económico e Social) in 1970 further consolidated this dissident 'liberal wing'.[6] Thus, despite the surprising action of the military, there were alternative elites who had close connections with various sectors of civil society, and who were ready to play a leading political role in the democratization process.

---

[4] Juan J. Linz and Alfred Stepan, *Problems of Democratic Transition and Consolidation: Southern Europe, South America and Post-Communist Europe* (Baltimore, MD: Johns Hopkins University Press, 1996), p. 117; Katherine Hite and Leonardo Morlino, 'Problematizing the Links between Authoritarian Legacies and "Good" Democracy', in *Authoritarian Legacies and Democracy in Latin America and Southern Europe*, ed. by Katherine Hite and Paola Cesarini (Notre Dame, IN: University of Notre Dame Press, 2004), pp. 25–83 (p. 47).
[5] Juan J. Linz, *Authoritarian and Totalitarian Regimes* (Boulder, CO: Lynne Rienner, 2000).
[6] Tiago Fernandes, *Nem ditadura nem revolução: a Ala Liberal no Marcelismo (1968–74)* (Lisbon: Dom Quixote, 2006).

Unlike Spain's *ruptura pactada*, Portugal experienced a transition without negotiations or pacts between the dictatorial elite and opposition forces. However, there is no direct causal link between this marked discontinuity and the subsequent radicalization: other transitions by rupture did not cause comparable crises of the state. As we will show below, the simultaneity of the democratization and decolonization processes was one factor of the crisis, while the latter was the main reason for the conflict in the immediate wake of the regime's collapse between some conservative generals and the Armed Forces Movement (MFA — Movimento das Forças Armadas) that had planned and executed the coup. This conflict was at the root of the military's generalized intervention in political life following the overthrow of the dictatorship.

The mobilization of diverse anti-dictatorial forces was crucial in the first days following the 1974 coup. It was especially important in the immediate dissolution of the most notorious institutions of the New State as well as in the occupation of various unions, corporatist organizations and municipalities. Some of the military elite, the leaders of some interest groups and a part of the 1st Provisional Government sought the rapid establishment of a presidentialist democratic regime following elections.

The institutionalization of the MFA transformed it into the dominant force behind the provisional governments. The interweaving of the MFA in the state's structures and its emergence as an authority for regulating conflicts, which substituted, dispersed and paralysed the classic mechanisms of legitimate state repression, prevented the recomposition of the state apparatus.[7] This was the main factor why, in the Portuguese case, the movement for the purging or dissolution of institutions exceeded those of classic transitions by rupture and, in many cases, became a component of the transgressing social movements.[8]

Indeed, the revolutionary period of 1974–75 was the most complex phase of the transition, if one considers the transition as the 'fluid and uncertain period in which democratic structures are emerging', but in which it is yet unclear what kind of regime is to be established.[9] During these two years, powerful tensions emerged within Portuguese society that did not begin to subside until 1976, with the approval of the new constitution and the holding of legislative and presidential elections.

The disagreements concerning the nature of decolonization, which was the initial driving force behind the conflict between the captains who had led the coup and General Spínola and other conservative generals, led to the emergence of the MFA as a political force. This then opened a space for social and political mobilization that exacerbated the crisis of the state, and which

---

[7] Diego Palacios Cerezales, *O poder caiu na rua: crise de Estado e acções colectivas na revolução portuguesa, 1974–75* (Lisbon: Imprensa de Ciências Sociais, 2003).
[8] Filipa Raimundo, 'Strategic Silence as a Third Way: Political Parties and Transitional Justice', *Democratization*, 22.6 (2015), 1054–71.
[9] Leonardo Morlino, *Democracy between Consolidation and Crisis: Parties, Groups and Citizens in Southern Europe* (Oxford: Oxford University Press, 1998), p. 19.

can perhaps explain why the moderate elites were incapable of directing the rapid institutionalization of democracy. Many analyses of the transition rightly emphasize the powerful 'revitalization of civil society' as a factor leading to the process of radicalization. As Philippe Schmitter notes: 'Portugal experienced one of the most intense and widespread mobilization experiences of any of the neo-democracies'.[10] It is important to note, however, that this mobilization developed in parallel with and in the presence of the protective cover of the MFA — indeed, it is difficult to imagine it developing in any other way.

The strength of the MFA, and of the military more generally, led to it exercising considerable leverage to ensure its inclusion in the nascent political system. Throughout that period, early attempts at the 'presidentialization' of the regime were quickly followed — after a failed coup attempt in March 1975 — with the first MFA–Political Parties pact about the future content of the constitution, signed two weeks before the scheduled elections to the Constituent Assembly in 1975. This pact gave the military a veto over the future constitutional text, severely limiting the work of the elected members of the Constituent Assembly, and even imposed the constitutionalization of an MFA assembly formed of officers, the role of which included participation in the indirect election of the head of state.

This was when the parties that were to represent the right and centre-right, the Social Democratic Centre (CDS — Centro Democrático Social) and the Popular Democratic Party (PPD — Partido Popular Democrático) were formed. The CDS, which incorporated sectors of Portuguese society that espoused conservative authoritarian values, was on the verge of being declared illegal right up until the eve of the elections to the Constituent Assembly on 25 April 1975.

As in other transitions to democracy, many political parties were formed or legalized after 25 April; however, most of the parties on the left of the political spectrum had existed clandestinely or semi-legally during the final years of the 'New State'. An example of this was the group of extreme left Maoist, Trotskyist, Guevarrist and Marxist parties. This was also the case of the PS, founded by Mário Soares in April 1973, and of the PCP, which was the oldest party in twentieth-century Portugal and which had existed clandestinely throughout the dictatorship period.[11]

More complex, and in many ways more difficult, was the creation of parties to represent the right of the political spectrum. Given legitimacy because of its roots in the 'liberal wing' of Marcelo Caetano's National Assembly and the clear opposition of its founder, Francisco Sá Carneiro, to the dictatorship, the PPD, which was created in the wake of 25 April, immediately took part in the provisional governments. Much more difficult was the life of the CDS, founded

---

[10] Philippe C. Schmitter, 'The Democratisation of Portugal in its Comparative Perspective', in *Portugal e a transição para a democracia, 1974–1976*, ed. by Fernando Rosas (Lisbon: Colibri, 1999), pp. 359–70 (p. 360).
[11] Marco Lisi, *Party Change, Recent Democracies, and Portugal: Comparative Perspectives* (Lanham, MD: Lexington Books, 2015).

by Diogo Freitas do Amaral, who was Marcelo Caetano's former assistant at the University of Lisbon law faculty and who had no history of opposition to the dictatorship. Following the prohibition of several right- and extreme-right-wing groups in 1974, these two parties attempted to exclude names associated with the New State and to find leaders with democratic legitimacy, while their political programmes tended to be to more to the left of their members and supporters. The MFA's decision to respect the electoral timetable was an important factor in the legitimation of the democratic regime, and the holding of these elections as scheduled helped strengthen the position of the moderate political parties.

Between 25 April 1974 and 25 April 1976 Portugal was led by provisional governments that reflected the dynamics of the crisis of Portuguese society and the growing dominance of the military and the various MFA factions, all of which resulted in several cleavages. The first of these concerned decolonization, which led to the downfall of General Spínola following the events of 28 September 1974 and the institutionalization of the MFA, which went on to lead the provisional governments. The second was between the moderates and radicals within the MFA, which was progressively accompanied by the anti-Communist stance of the PS and the parties of the centre-right on the one side, and the PCP and some left-wing groups on the other.

While the conflict between António de Spínola and the MFA was mainly over the colonial question, the Palma Carlos coup at the very beginning of the transition sought to bring about the swift legitimization of the new regime, while proposing presidential elections to take place in October 1974 and the simultaneous approval of a provisional constitution.[12] The elections to the Constituent Assembly were planned for the end of 1976, almost one and a half years after the presidential elections.[13] As Diogo Freitas do Amaral noted: 'the MFA was to be dissolved, Spínola's personal authority was to be greatly enhanced and the regime would define itself in practice as "Gaullist presidentialism".'[14]

Supported by parties of the left, but largely on its own initiative, the MFA moved away from Spínola, both because of his attempts to be the effective leader in the process of institutionalizing democracy and over his colonial policy. With the appointment of the 2nd Provisional Government, the MFA launched its independent organization, the CR, and it was by their hand that Spínola promulgated Law 7/74, which gave the colonies the right to independence, determined the legal framework that would allow decolonization, and defined the organizations that would be involved in the process. In the summer of 1974 Spínola persisted with his call for a referendum, seeking an alternative to the liberation movements and raising the hopes of the white population in the colonies — especially in Angola and Mozambique — much against the dominant view within the new party system, and the MFA, which was

[12] Luís Nuno Rodrigues, *Spínola: uma biografia* (Lisbon: Esfera dos Livros, 2010).
[13] Maria Inácia Rezola, *25 de Abril: mitos de uma revolução* (Lisbon: Esfera dos Livros, 2007).
[14] Diogo Freitas do Amaral, *O Antigo Regime e a Revolução: memórias políticas (1941–1975)* (Lisbon: Bertrand, 1995), p. 212.

calling for a swift transition to independence. The victory of the MFA on the decolonization issue led to Spínola's resignation in September 1974.

The defeat of the pro-Spínola forces and his exile following the attempted coup of 11 March 1975, and the MFA's turn to the left, with the introduction of agrarian reform and the nationalization of large Portuguese companies, were both symbols and drivers of an accentuated state crisis that fed powerful social movements. The MFA established the Conselho da Revolução and concluded several agreements with the political parties that gave it a dominant position. The MFA's decision to respect the electoral timetable was a crucial factor in the establishment of the democratic regime's founding legitimacy, and the elections of 25 April 1975 gave the moderate parties powerful leverage. The decision to opt for a d'Hondt system of proportional representation was the result of a determination to ensure that as many parties as possible were represented, with a bonus for the largest party.

The First MFA–Political Party Pact and the Elections to the Constituent Assembly

The immediate holding of free elections to a body that would design a new constitution was a common demand in almost all Third Wave democratization processes.[15] Nevertheless, both the nature of the transition and the conditionality of political forces greatly altered this ever-present demand (see Fig. 1).

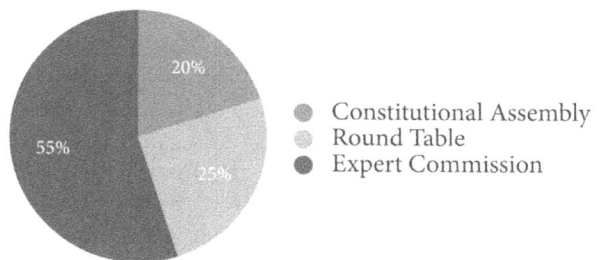

FIG. 1. Types of Constitution-Making, 1945–2004 (%)
Source: Braulio Gómez Fortes, *O controlo político dos processos constituintes: os casos de Espanha e Portugal* (Lisbon: Imprensa de Ciências Sociais, 2009), p. 12.

As we saw above, the Palma Carlos project sought to create a powerful president. This project was supported by the leader of the PPD, Francisco Sá Carneiro; however, the PS insisted on an immediate election to a Constituent Assembly, even as it continued to recognize the revolutionary hegemony of the MFA. The PCP was fiercely opposed to General Spínola's constitutional decree

---

[15] Braulio Gómez Fortes, *O controlo político dos processos constituintes: os casos de Espanha e Portugal* (Lisbon: Imprensa de Ciências Sociais, 2009).

project, more because of its conservative nature that for its confidence in a Constitutional Assembly. It was aware that its electoral force in the elections to the Constituent Assembly could be weak, reducing its influence over any future constitution.

Even before 11 March 1975 the MFA had opened negotiations on a constitutional pact with the political parties. Its main goal was to ensure its political and institutional survival. The moderate parties, especially the PS, had early expressed their preference for elections to a Constituent Assembly such as had been proposed and reaffirmed by the MFA. At its first congress, in December 1974, the PS approved a motion stating that the Constituent Assembly must be the result of the 'expression of the will of the Portuguese people'. Despite the tensions between the PCP and the MFA, the PS accepted the first MFA–Political Parties pact, convinced its eventual electoral victory would give it political legitimacy.

The PS demonstrated its willingness to compromise with the demands for the MFA's institutionalization, out of a fear it might turn against the parties. For its part, the PCP was the leading supporter of limiting the powers of the Constituent Assembly. Jorge Miranda, former PSD deputy to the Constituent Assembly, recalled that the parties signed the first constitutional platform 'solely to ensure elections were held'.[16] Part of the pact signed by the parties on 11 April 1975 had already been negotiated before 11 March and had been worked on by constitutionalists to include the most ideological dimension of the implantation of socialism and the reference to sovereign bodies.[17]

As Gómez Fortes notes: 'the final limits to the organization of political power were of an intensity unknown in western democracies until then'. On the one hand, it was established that 'the terms of this platform must incorporate the political constitution being prepared by the Constituent Assembly'.[18] The CR's power of veto was extensive: 'elaborated and approved by the Constituent Assembly, the new Constitution had to be promulgated by the President of the Republic and approved by the Council of the Revolution'.[19] On the other hand, the actions of the Constituent Assembly were limited to preparing the constitution: it had no legislative authority.

While the political parties were calling for the direct election of the President, the pact signed between the MFA and the parties proposed an electoral college that consisted of the future parliament and the MFA Assembly.[20] In this way, the MFA imposed upon the parties a 'platform for a constitutional agreement' in exchange for holding elections to the Constitutional Assembly. To guarantee

---

[16] Fortes, p. 180.
[17] V. Moreira, 'A edificação do novo sistema constitucional democrático', in *Portugal Contemporâneo*, ed. by A. Reis, 6 vols (Lisbon: Publicações Alfa, 1993), III, 170–83.
[18] Fortes, p. 234.
[19] Rezola, *25 de Abril: mitos de uma revolução*, p. 158.
[20] Maria Inácia Rezola, *O Conselho da Revolução e a transição para a democracia em Portugal, 1974-1976* (Lisbon: Campo da Comunicação, 2006).

that its interests were protected under the new constitution, the MFA reserved two sovereign bodies to itself: the CR and the Armed Forces Assembly. The CR enjoyed extensive political powers, including control over the constitutionality of law and a monopoly on all legislation affecting the military. The pact ensured that regardless of the result of the elections to the Constitutional Assembly the CR retained leadership of the process throughout the transitional period and would be declared a sovereign body within the future constitution. The celebration of the Constitutional Agreement between the MFA and the political parties on 11 April 1975 gave the CR the guarantees it required to ensure the Constituent Assembly did not exceed the principles outlined in the MFA's programme and that it respected all the 'revolutionary victories' already achieved.

The first democratic elections in Portuguese history were won by the moderate parties, with the PS emerging as the leading political party in the country, followed by the PPD (Table 1).

TABLE 1: Electoral Results for the Constituent Assembly, 25-4-1975
Source: Comissão Nacional de Eleições.

Party	Mandates	% of votes
PS - Partido Socialista	116	37.87
PPD - Partido Popular Democrático	81	26.39
PCP - Partido Comunista Português	30	12.46
CDS - Centro Democrático Social	16	7.61
MDP - Movimento Democrático Português	5	4.14
FSP - Frente Socialista Popular	0	1.16
MES - Movimento Esquerda Socialista	0	1.02
UDP - União Democrática Popular	1	0.79
FEC - Frente Eleitoral dos Comunistas	0	0.58
PPM - Partido Popular Monárquico	0	0.57
PUP - Partido de Unidade Popular	0	0.23
LCI - Liga Comunista Internacionalista	0	0.19
ADIM - Associação para a Defesa dos Interesses de Macau	1	0.03
CDM - Centro Democrático de Macau	0	0.02
Invalid votes		6.95
Total	250	100%

The Constituent Assembly that emerged from the elections on 25 April 1975 could not be easily controlled by the MFA because of the poor results achieved by the parties closest to it. After 11 March 1975, some elements of the MFA could no longer hide their hitherto discreet support for either the PCP or the MDP. Nevertheless, the 12% of the vote won by the Communists and their allies put them in the minority within the Constituent Assembly.

With nearly 38% of the vote, the PS was the clear winner of this election. When the Constituent Assembly opened, the PS was already in open opposition to the policies of the MFA and of the 5th Provisional Government led by Vasco Gonçalves.[21] The PS used the first day of debate in the assembly to reduce the limits on constitutional powers contained within the MFA–Political Parties pact. Mário Soares recalled: 'The elections radically changed the country's political landscape. The popular vote gave a new legitimacy to the Socialist Party. From that moment we were invested with the popular will'.[22]

The second winner of the elections was the PPD which, despite the hostile atmosphere against the right and despite its manifesto being much further to the left than its electorate, won 26%. While the PPD and PS combined accounted for almost 70% of the electorate and held an overwhelming majority of seats, it was not until after 25 November 1975 that they succeeded in recovering some of the powers they sought for the Constituent Assembly elected on 25 April 1975.

Radicalization, 'Hot Summer' and Constitution

It is too simplistic to consider the 'hot summer' of 1975 as simply an attempt by the Portuguese Communist Party (PCP — Partido Comunista Português) to impose a new dictatorship, with the support of the Soviet Union. Naturally, the democratic political elite made much of this argument in its founding discourse, but this does not provide a full explanation of events. The situation was more complex: conflict was fed by the development of strong grassroots political organizations such as the workers' commissions, the growing challenge posed by the extreme left during the crisis, and its influence within the military. The importance of divisions within the armed forces in driving these events forward means they cannot be explained as part of a 'programmed conspiracy'.

Portuguese society began to polarize in the summer of 1975, with the emergence of an anti-revolutionary (and anti-Communist) movement in the north of the country. The PS and PPD backed the moderates, leading demonstrations in Lisbon and Porto, with the former opening a schism with the Communists that was to become a central divide on the left of the political spectrum. In the provinces to the north of the Tagus, the hierarchy of the Catholic Church and local notables supported parish-level mobilizations, with the local military authorities either remaining neutral or being complicit in

---

[21] Maria Manuela Cruzeiro, *Vasco Gonçalves: um General na Revolução* (Lisbon: Editorial Notícias, 2002).
[22] Mário Soares, *Um político assume-se* (Lisbon: Temas e Debates, 2010), p. 180.

their activities. As elements of the extreme-right and the right, military officers and civilians alike, began to mobilize, the anti-left offensive became violent, with attacks on the offices of the PCP, groups of the extreme-left and associated unions (Fig. 2). Right-wing terrorist organizations emerged, such as the Democratic Movement for the Liberation of Portugal (MDLP — Movimento Democrático para a Liberação de Portugal) and the Portuguese Liberation Army (ELP — Exército para a Libertação de Portugal).[23]

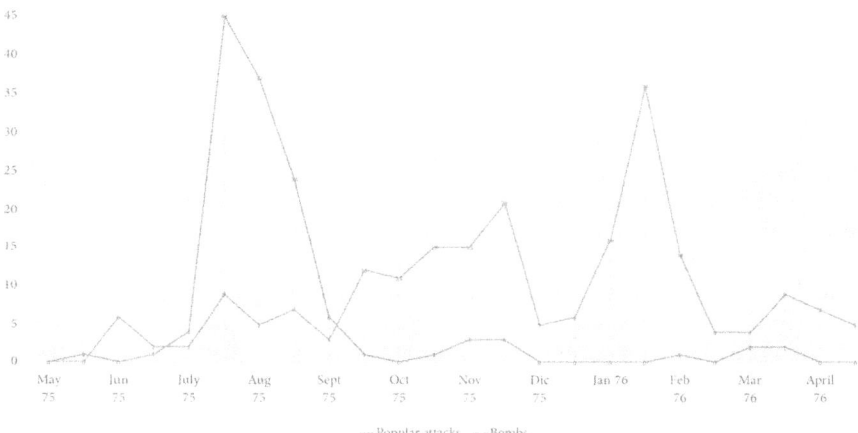

FIG. 2. Popular vs clandestine anticommunist violence, 1975–76
Source: Diego Palacios Cerezales, 'Confrontación, violencia política y democratización: Portugal 1975', *Política y Sociedad*, 40.3 (2003), 189–213.

Although supported by centre-right parties, it was Mário Soares's PS that was responsible for the political polarization and anti-Communist offensive in 1975, and which also received the greatest political and strategic international support. Some campaigns were emblematic of this time, such as the noted denunciation of the occupation of the PS-supporting *República* newspaper by left-wing journalists, which was to have serious international repercussions as they were denounced as PCP supporters. Another significant event at this time was the occupation of Radio Renascença, the Catholic Church's broadcaster, by left-wing activists. The PS and PPD walked out of the provisional government they had joined following the 1974 coup, and the PS broke away from the MFA as Mário Soares demanded the dismissal of the Prime Minister, Vasco Gonçalves, who had formed the 5th Provisional Government in July 1975 without involvement of either PS or PPD. It was in the context of this growing

[23] Diego Palacios Cerezales, 'Confrontación, violencia política y democratización: Portugal 1975', *Política y Sociedad*, 4.3 (2003), 189–213; Riccardo Marchi, 'The Portuguese Radical Right in the Democratic Period', in *Mapping the Extreme Right in Contemporary Europe*, ed. by Andrea Mammone, Emmanuel Godin and Brian Jenkins (London: Routledge, 2012), pp. 95–108.

mobilization that in August 1975 a moderate wing emerged in the MFA: the Group of Nine, which distanced itself from the 5th Provisional Government led by Vasco Gonçalves.

In 1974–75 Portugal experienced significant foreign intervention both in diplomatic terms and in the formation of political parties, unions and interest organizations, as well as in the shaping of the anti-left strategy that evolved over the 'hot summer' of 1975. The Portuguese case was a divisive issue in international organizations, within the North Atlantic Treaty Organization (NATO) and the European Economic Community (EEC), affecting relations between these two organizations and the eastern bloc countries led by the Soviet Union.[24] All evidence makes it clear that in 1974–75 Portugal was an issue of 'international importance'.

Taken by surprise by the coup, the international community, particularly the United States, focused on supporting democratic political forces of the centre-left and right in Portugal, as well as on intervening in the rapid process of decolonization, particularly in Angola.[25] The same post-Second World War methods deployed to deal with Italy were used in Portugal. The moderate political parties were financed by the US administration, which together with the international organizations of the European 'political families' — these often mediating the US role — also supported the training of party cadres. Although domestic political factors played a critical role in enabling both the triumph of moderate civilian forces and the final withdrawal of the military from the political arena, international support and the prospect of EEC membership was more important than the early literature on the transition suggests.

The General Workers' Union (UGT — União Geral de Trabalhadores), created by the PS and PSD as a counterbalance to the Communist-dominated General Confederation of Portuguese Workers — National Intersyndical (CGTP-IN — Confederação Geral dos Trabalhadores Portugueses — Intersindical Nacional), received a lot of external financial and training support.[26] While the Communists received considerable support from the Soviet Union and Eastern Europe, this was easily outweighed by Western support to the moderates.

Caught between the pressures exerted by the extreme left associated with Otelo Saraiva de Carvalho's COPCON (Comando Operacional do Continente) and by the Group of Nine, Vasco Gonçalves's 5th Provisional Government resigned at the beginning of September and was replaced by the 6th Provisional Government, made up of moderate officers and the PS and PPD. This government was immediately placed under pressure by the extreme left and was mistrusted by the PCP. Tensions between moderates and the military and civilian left continued to grow, leading to some of the most significant episodes,

[24] Tiago Moreira de Sá and Bernardino Gomes, *Carlucci vs Kissinger: os EUA e a Revolução Portuguesa* (Lisbon: D. Quixote, 2008).
[25] Tiago Moreira de Sá, *Os Estados Unidos e a descolonização de Angola* (Lisbon: Dom Quixote, 2011).
[26] Rui Mateus, *Contos proibidos: memórias de um PS desconhecido* (Lisbon: D. Quixote, 1996).

including the siege of the Constituent Assembly by a demonstration of civil construction workers at the beginning of November 1975.

With the last-minute withdrawal of the PCP on 25 November 1975 the moderates eliminated the radical left. It was in this context of polarization that from June to November 1975 the basis of the Constitution was discussed and negotiated by the Constituent Assembly.

The Constituent Assembly and the Hot Summer of 1975

The Constituent Assembly met for the first time on 9 June 1975 under strict instructions, in accordance with the MFA-approved agreement, to consider only the drafting of a constitution; however, its first challenge was to establish a time before the Order of the Day during which deputies could debate the national and international political situation. Article 42 of its Regulations allowed deputies to express their political views before the constitutional debates began.[27] This additional political aspect was possible largely because of united action by the PS and PPD, which had effectively formed a national political alliance.

The length of time before the Order of the Day was, in principle, one hour, although that could be extended with the approval of a majority of deputies. At the moments of greatest tension during the 'hot summer', this time was used to defend the electoral legitimacy of the Constituent Assembly, just as the representatives of the parties closest to the 5th Provisional Government and the MFA feared. According to Freitas do Amaral, then leader of the CDS: 'the work of the assembly started slowly and the atmosphere was very tense'.[28] On several occasions, the Constituent Assembly was accused of going beyond its remit, with denunciations noting that instead of working to draft a new constitution it was spending too much time criticizing the government. The PS was most guilty of seeking to enhance the Constituent Assembly's parliamentary legitimacy against the radical left and its 'revolutionary legitimacy'. For example, in August 1975 a communiqué from the PS National Commission stated that, 'as a consequence of the divisions within the MFA', the Constituent Assembly had become the true seat of 'national sovereignty'.[29] However, at the same time as it was being used to support the external political struggle, divisions between the Communist minority and the MFA were less accentuated during discussions on the future Constitution.

The Constituent Assembly began working on constitutional projects, carefully respecting the limits imposed on it through the 'first platform of constitutional agreement' signed with the MFA.[30] Given the PS and PPD had a

---

[27] <http://app.parlamento.pt/LivrosOnLine/Vozes_Constituinte/med01200000j.html#conteudo>.
[28] Amaral, p. 390.
[29] Jornal Novo, 12 August 1975, p. 2.
[30] Maria Inácia Rezola, 'O Movimento das Forças Armada e a Assembleia Constituinte na Revolução

majority in the assembly, they determined its organization in the face of PCP opposition. According to the regulations, each parliamentary group submitted its constitutional proposals. Seven commissions were established — one for each chapter of the constitution — to examine all submitted projects. More importantly, the composition of each commission strictly reflected each group's share of representation in the Assembly. Each commission was made up of four PS deputies, three from the PPD, two from the PCP and one each from the CDS and MDP/DE, with the Popular Democratic Union (UDP — União Democrática Popular) having one observer. The projects submitted by all political parties respected the organization of political power defined by the MFA–Political Parties pact and, importantly, the commissions reflected the overwhelming majority enjoyed by the PS and PPD.

Observation of the work carried out by the commissions during the 'hot summer' makes it possible to conclude that the members and commissions enjoyed considerable autonomy in the face of the divisions at the national level. First, with the PS being the dominant party in the Assembly and with many of the constitutional principles being approved by a simple majority, its parliamentary group respected the weight of each party. Second, and perhaps more important, many of the constitutional projects were more similar than one might have thought given the external divisions between the PS, the parties of the centre-right and the PCP. The third factor also concerns the significant autonomy, mainly within the PS and PSD, between the deputies and parliamentary groups and their respective leaderships. In the PCP, however, there was more centralized control between deputies and the parliamentary group's leadership in the Constituent Assembly. On the other hand, the deputies, while co-ordinated by their parliamentary groups, also enjoyed considerable freedom to negotiate, deliberate and compromise within the commissions.[31] This dynamic also meant that the exact content of the constitution, to the extent that party sources allow us to observe, was not a priority for the PS or the PSD during this difficult period of Portuguese democratization.

The many constitutional projects, and especially those of the PS and the parties of the centre-right, displayed a well-studied trend favouring a swing to the left that was also expressed in their political manifestos.[32] The agreements with the MFA also partially explain the principles behind the collectivization of the means of production or the path towards a classless society; however, this was not the case with social rights, for example, the commission for which met between August and October 1975, and other examples that could be given.

Portuguesa', *Historia Constitucional*, 13 (2012), 635–59.
[31] Mónica Brito Vieira and Filipe Carreira da Silva, *O momento constituinte: os direitos sociais na Constituição* (Coimbra: Almedina, 2010).
[32] Maritheresa Frain, *PPD/PSD e a consolidação do regime democrático* (Lisbon: Editorial Notícias, 1998); Carlos Jalali, *Partidos e democracia em Portugal, 1974-2005: da revolução ao bipartidarismo?* (Lisbon: Imprensa de Ciências Sociais, 2007).

As the most important study of social rights in the Constituent Assembly illustrates, the goal of constitutionally consecrating the institutions of a well-established welfare state was common to all parties, which is clear when analysing the respective constitutional projects: 'Not only were social rights present in all the projects, they were all substantially the same. All the projects described these rights with a very similar precision and detailed the institutions and policies required to bring them about'.[33] The PS was thus shaping the work of the commission, looking at the articles of the different party projects more or less in proportion to their electoral weight. At some points making concessions to the left (many, and partially to its own deputies), at others to its right (few, but raising some contradictions), it behaved like the ruling party. The result, in the words of academic analysts, was 'an amalgamation of utopian expectations of a poor country going through a social and political revolution'.[34]

From 25 November 1975 to the 1976 Constitution

After the 25 November 1975 coup had neutralized the radical-left military wing and placed the PCP in political isolation, a new agreement was negotiated between the parties and the military: the second MFA–Political Party pact. This document included the direct election of the President of the Republic but under strict conditions imposed by the moderates within the MFA who now held power. Among these conditions was the 'implicit military clause', by which the PS and the PPD supported a military candidate to be chosen by the CR through an internal consultation process in the coming presidential elections.[35]

The coup of 25 November represented the irreversible victory of the Group of Nine, whose ideology was more moderate and closer to the PS and which recognized the democratic legitimacy of the Constituent Assembly. The institutionalization of the CR and other items on the agenda of civil–military relations remained, as did the matter of the election of the President. However, no other aspects of the constitution being debated in the Constituent Assembly were of great concern to either the parties or the CR.

On 2 December 1975, the PPD presented a proposal to the Constituent Assembly for the revision of the first platform; however, the PS was opposed. Now that the MFA was prepared to review the pact, the PS took up the initiative again and on 11 December 1975 the Constituent Assembly, in the face of PCP opposition, proposed a revision of the pact. The proposal of the PS included the election of the President by direct suffrage.

---

[33] Vieira and da Silva, p. 31.
[34] Filipe Carreira da Silva and Mónica Brito Vieira, 'Direitos sociais na Constituição: uma análise da constitucionalização dos direitos sociais em Portugal, 1975–76', *Relações Internacionais*, 49 (2016), 69–94 (p. 87).
[35] André Gonçalves Pereira, *O Semipresidencialismo em Portugal* (Lisbon: Ática, 1984), p. 42.

In January 1976 the CR made an official request to the parties for their proposals. The PS and PSD no longer formed a front, which many believe was the result of their setting out their stalls for the upcoming legislative elections. The PPD wanted to separate itself politically from the PS, which was broadly considered the winner on 25 November 1975. While it drafted the constitution, it was also preparing for the coming elections and the PPD, which was a minority in the Constituent Assembly, attempted to use the negotiations on the platform to get approval for those of its proposals that were more difficult to get through.

Given its strategic proximity to the CR, the PS thought it needed it to ensure military discipline and to guarantee the future consolidation of democracy. It is also worth noting that within both parties there were tendencies favouring putting more distance between them and the CR and who opposed the prerogatives it continued to impose over the civilian political elite.

The outcome of this story is well known. The final proposal for the revision of the first pact, based on a suggestion by the PS, was the successful proposal to directly elect the President. The negotiations on the second pact signed by all the political parties on 26 February 1976 have been extensively studied and debated.[36] The Constituent Assembly had to comply with the externally agreed limits and to approve a constitution in which the military power was not subordinate to civilian power and in which the CR survived. The CR used an internal process to choose a military candidate for President. The famous 'implicit military clause' contained in the second pact was a fact.[37] To ensure laws were constitutional, a Constitutional Commission was created to act as a consultative body for the CR. The pact included the transitory nature of the CR as a sovereign body.

One topic that emerged between 25 November and the approval of the new constitution was the call for a referendum of ratification. The PPD wanted a referendum that would allow partial liberation from the limitations established in 1975. Some of the PPD's leaders publicly declared that 'the constitution is full of Marxist principles that it is unlikely the Portuguese people will accept'.[38] In the meantime, the PS distanced itself from this proposal, because — according to some studies — it feared the PPD could come to occupy the 'political centre'.[39] In the end, there was no referendum and the constitution was ratified by the Constituent Assembly. Once the constitution was approved, with the abstention of the CDS, most of its principles were accepted with little tension — certainly

---

[36] Miguel Galvão Teles, 'A segunda plataforma de acordo constitucional entre o Movimento das Forças Armadas e os partidos políticos', in *Perspectivas Constitucionais: nos 20 anos da Constituição de 1976*, ed. by Jorge Miranda, 3 vols (Coimbra: Coimbra Editora, 1998), III, 54–69.
[37] Pedro Santana Lopes and José Manuel Durão Barroso, *Sistema de governo e sistema partidário* (Amadora: Bertrand, 1980); André Freire and António Costa Pinto, *O poder presidencial em Portugal* (Lisbon: Dom Quixote, 2005).
[38] Fortes, p. 270.
[39] Fortes. p. 271.

less tension than the legacy of civil–military relations in the consolidation of Portuguese democracy.

Conclusions

In interpreting the contents of the 1976 Portuguese Constitution — its accentuated left-wing position in particular — there are three factors that need to be highlighted: the powerful role of the military in relation to the Constitutional Assembly; the clear turn to the left in the programmes of the political parties; and the impact in the Constitutional Assembly of the external political radicalization in 1975.

As expected, the Portuguese constitution was determined by the nature of the transition, while officers organized within the MFA were determining agents in the contents of the 1976 Constitution who even attempted to grant themselves the exclusive right to promulgate the new constitution. Despite keeping its promise to call an election to a Constituent Assembly, through the first and second constitutional agreements as the beginning and end of the process of preparing a constitution, it established powerful conditions on the design of Portuguese democracy. Nevertheless, these conditions referred mainly to the role of the MFA and the CR in shaping political institutions and in the manner of electing the President of the Republic and the President's relationship with the military.

The nature of the transition, the stigmatization of the authoritarian past, and the crisis of the state undoubtedly affected the birth of the political parties representing the centre-right and right, but the turn to the left was a feature of all parties during this period, including the PCP and the PS. The many constitutional projects, and especially those of the PS and the parties of the centre-right, illustrate this shift to the left in their political manifestos.

Observation of the work carried out by the commissions during the 'hot summer' of 1975 makes it possible to conclude that the members and commissions enjoyed considerable independence of action in the face of the cleavages across the national political field, which was complemented by the relative independence of deputies within the commissions when faced with the divisions at the national level.

Although with significant tensions, there was a strong convergence and the PS — the dominant party in the Constituent Assembly — largely respected the weight of each party and gave the deputies a significant degree of independence. This dynamic also meant that some ideological dimensions of the constitution were not a priority for either the PS or PPD during this difficult period of Portuguese democratization. This factor is perhaps the most important in the apparent irony of the 'losers' of democratic consolidation being transformed, just a short while later, into the main guardians of the constitution that was approved in 1976.

The Cooperative Movement in Portugal beyond the Revolution: Housing Cooperatives between Shifting Tides

CAMILA RODRIGUES AND TIAGO FERNANDES

Departamento de Estudos Políticos, Universidade NOVA de Lisboa

Introduction

This essay analyses the development of the housing cooperative movement in Portugal, from the revolutionary transition to democracy up to the present day. Cooperatives present a particular characteristic which differentiates them from associations:[1] they are voluntary associations that develop an economic activity. As such, they are civil society organizations that have both social and economic functions and are 'bounded and constrained' by market dynamics.[2] In contemporary Portugal, housing cooperatives have been facing many obstacles, as a result of the successive economic policies of the Portuguese governments after 1976 and the demands of European integration that gradually eroded the legacy of the 1974 revolution.

During the *Estado Novo*, housing policies were an instrument of social control and reinforcement of hierarchical relations. The working classes were spread throughout the suburbs, which prevented their concentration and the dangers they might pose to governmental stability.[3] This housing discrimination was aggravated by the intense rural exodus that in the middle of the last century brought many workers from small villages to the industrial cities. Social housing programmes were scarce, scattered and of a strongly symbolic, disciplinary and selective nature; they were mostly aimed at particular social and professional groups that complied with the dominant moral standards.[4]

The revolution presented an opportunity for neighbourhood movements,

---

[1] The essay deals with cooperatives in general and not with specific typologies, since the data collected does not distinguish national from regional cooperatives or service from member-owned cooperatives.
[2] Gianpaolo Baiocchi, Patrick Heller and Marcelo Silva, *Bootstrapping Democracy: Transforming Local Governance and Civil Society in Brazil* (Stanford, CA: Stanford University Press, 2011), p. 26.
[3] João Queirós, 'Estratégias e discursos políticos em torno da reabilitação de centros urbanos: considerações exploratórias a partir do caso do Porto', *Sociologia: Problemas e Práticas*, 55 (2007), 91–116.
[4] Marielle Christine Gros, 'Pequena história do alojamento social em Portugal', *Sociedade e Território*, 20 (1994), 80–90.

which were empowered in a context of state fragility and redefinition of hierarchical structures. It was a period of intense neighbourhood mobilization. Neighbourhood commissions were constituted spontaneously or with the support of the Movement of the Armed Forces (MFA), with the objective of increasing the level of civic participation in the management of neighbourhoods. One of the most controversial initiatives was the occupation of vacant houses, both public and private, with the objective of providing a home for the most disadvantaged and also of creating welfare and recreational resources for the community. The activity of the commissions decreased significantly after November 1975, because the victorious moderate forces required that governmental decisions prevail over popular initiative.

The approval of the Portuguese Constitution in April 1976 marked the demise of the most radical left-wing political forces. The Constitution still kept faith with the revolutionary spirit, espousing 'the transition to socialism through the creation of conditions for the democratic exercise of the power by the working classes'.[5] The right to housing remained enshrined in the constitution, but this disposition faded gradually in the context of a capitalist liberal democracy of European inspiration.

This process led to an individualization of the right to housing, which affected neighbourhood movements: there was an evolution from collective mobilization to individual solutions.[6] However, the close of the critical juncture that had favoured popular mobilization was not the end of neighbourhood organizations in Portugal. They persisted in the context of the consolidation of liberal democracy and sought new strategies of survival and areas of intervention. Neighbourhood participation acquired new contours, but it did not revert to the insignificance it had presented during the fascist regime.

Background

Following a brief period of participatory frenzy during and immediately after the revolution, social housing movements evolved from revolutionary enthusiasm into a mature organizational posture, aimed at aggregating collective interests and representing them in a consolidated democracy. This process entailed a reduction in the number of neighbourhood organizations constituted each year, which now took two forms: housing cooperatives and neighbourhood associations. In the early 1980s, the number continued to decrease but later in the decade they regained some vitality. It is possible to observe that the constitution of new neighbourhood associations has stabilized in the present day, but the constitution of housing cooperatives shows a consistent decline

---

[5] All the translations were made by the authors.
[6] Charles Downs, 'Residents' Commissions and Urban Struggles in Revolutionary Portugal', in *In Search of Modern Portugal: The Revolution and its Consequences*, ed. by Laurence Graham and Douglas Wheeler (Madison: University of Wisconsin Press, 1983), pp. 151–80.

in most sectors. Looking at the housing organizational sector — housing cooperatives and neighbourhood associations — we observe that it follows a general pattern, as shown in Fig. 1:

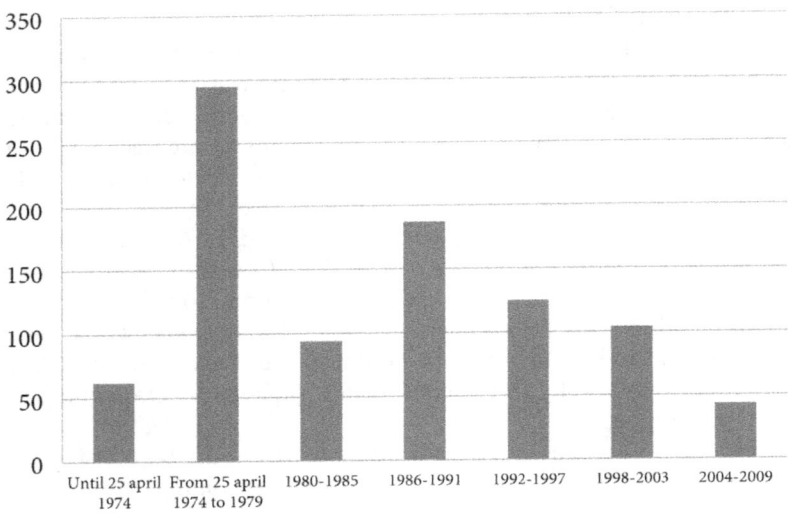

FIG. 1: Cooperatives. Sources:[7] 'Civil Society and Democracy: Portugal in a Comparative Perspective' and *Livro Branco do SAAL*

The situation displayed by the graphic, which concerns only housing *cooperatives*, is easily placed in its wider context. Still a markedly rural country right up to the 1960s, only lightly industrialized and with a powerful Catholic Church,[8] Portugal did not go through the Industrial Revolution as strongly as some other European countries, where the working class combatted oppressive working conditions to claim its civil rights. Throughout the nineteenth century, cooperatives were scarce but they made their presence felt and were seen benevolently as supportive forms of production that had the potential to improve the living conditions of the most deprived social classes. In 1867, cooperatives acquired legal autonomy from the commercial sector with the

---

[7] This data is provided by the project 'Civil Society and Democracy: Portugal in a Comparative Perspective', based at the Department of Political Studies of the Universidade NOVA de Lisboa and coordinated by Pedro Tavares de Almeida, Tiago Fernandes and Rui Branco. The National Record of Collective Entities gathers data on organizations that still existed or were created after 1978. As such, it misses some more ephemeral organizations created and dissolved in the heat of the revolution, such as organizations related with the Ambulatory Local Support Service (SAAL — Serviço de Apoio Ambulatório Local). To overcome this limitation we complemented it with data from the White Book of the SAAL (*Livro Branco do SAAL*), a collection of raw documents from that programme. We did not include in this graphic the extinctions because their number is very low, suggesting that it may be inflated by 'ghost' organizations that were not formally deactivated but in reality no longer function.
[8] Carlota Quintão, 'O terceiro sector e a sua renovação em Portugal: uma abordagem preliminar', *IS Working Papers*, 2 (2011), 1–18.

publication of the 'Andrade Corvo' law, which defined them as associations aimed at promoting mutual support among their partners. This political measure, together with a reinforcement of mutual aid associations, initially envisaged the strengthening of the social economy as a whole but later on, due to the relative failure of a federalist approach to the sector, it became a part of an effort to deepen the various cooperative and associative branches.[9]

This understanding of the autonomous nature of cooperatives suffered a setback with the Commercial Code, published in 1888, which constituted, for almost a century, the legal framework for the cooperative sector. Cooperatives were understood as a sub-species of traditional commercial companies,[10] thus losing their solidarity and not-for-profit character and becoming commercial agents like any others.[11] Despite this setback, the number of cooperatives increased more than fivefold during the First Republic (1910-26), and by 1926 there were 336 organizations active in the cooperative sector. This increase was due to the support granted to the sector, for although the Republic was paternalistic and failed to create a consistent and integrated legal framework, it viewed cooperatives as a way to improve the living conditions of the working classes, thus serving a purpose of social control: they contributed to decreasing the risks associated with poverty and they limited social protest.[12]

The *Estado Novo* maintained an ambiguous relationship with cooperatives. The rural policy of the regime promoted agricultural cooperatives as instruments of economic regulation and wage control. Consumer and cultural cooperatives were repressed due to their proletarian social basis, which was regarded as a potential source of political instability. The general tendency was to repress the cooperative sector and the fragmentation of its branches was an unavoidable consequence.[13] In 1971, new legislation determined that cooperatives were similar to associations, unless their activity was exclusively economic and in the interest of their members. This legal measure extended to the cooperative sector the restrictions already felt by associations, which in turn motivated protest movements, thus leading to the extinction of the most troublesome cooperatives.

---

[9] Ferreira da Costa 'Nota histórica sobre o cooperativismo português', in *Cooperativismo, emprego e economia social*, ed. by Carlos Pestana Barros and J. C. Gomes Santos (Lisbon: Vulgata: 1999), pp. 17-26.
[10] José António Rodrigues, 'O quadro jurídico do cooperativismo português', in *Cooperativismo, emprego e economia social*, ed. by Carlos Pestana Barros and J. C. Gomes Santos (Lisbon: Vulgata: 1999), pp. 121-36.
[11] Hélder Cardoso Pereira, *Associativismo e capital social: perfil sociológico dos dirigentes das cooperativas de consumo em Portugal* (Lisbon: Editora Campo da Comunicação, 2012).
[12] Rui Namorado, 'Cooperativismo e política em Portugal', in *Cooperativismo, emprego e economia social*, ed. by Carlos Pestana Barros and J. C. Gomes Santos (Lisbon: Vulgata: 1999), pp. 87-120.
[13] Ferreira da Costa, 'Nota histórica'.

Housing Cooperatives beyond the Revolution

The social revolution of 1974–75 created the opportunity for long-repressed social forces to express themselves, initially in an informal and spontaneous way, and later in an organized and institutional manner. In 1975, the Commission for Cooperative Support was created to coordinate the public services responsible for the study and management of the cooperative sector. The António Sérgio Institute for the Cooperative Sector (INSCOOP) was constituted a year later as a public institute designed to support the sector. The cooperative sector was assumed as a fundamental element in the democratic transition, 'fostering and intensifying the global productive capacity' and 'creating employment' (Decree-Law no. 249/75 of 4 July 1975).

The new Constitution of the Portuguese Republic, approved in April 1976, understood the cooperative sector as a cornerstone in the development of social property and determined the right to the free constitution of cooperatives and the state's responsibility to grant them fiscal and financial benefits, favourable credit conditions and technical support. In 1980, the Cooperative Code was published to finally align legislation with the constitution.[14] It laid down a high degree of autonomy for the cooperative sector in relation to all civil and commercial law that regulated other organizational forms, and in its final formulation, in agreement with the International Cooperative Alliance (ICA), it understood cooperatives as collective autonomous organizations aimed at satisfying the needs of their members according to a logic of cooperation.[15]

This was a period that saw different perspectives emerging on the role cooperatives played in Portuguese democracy, perspectives that could be identified in both political agents and cooperative managers. As the manager of an umbrella organization operating in the cooperative sector has stated, there are cooperative leaders 'from left to right'.[16] However, the understanding of the role played by the cooperative movement differed substantially: if the moderate right-wing parties understood the cooperative sector as a solution to specific problems, and never as a possible alternative model for the economy, the Communists envisaged a transition to socialism through the cooperative sector.[17] In spite of the political support granted to cooperatives, such conflicting perspectives, and the priority given to membership of the European Economic Community (EEC), led to a certain inertia in the development of the cooperative sector in the late 1970s and early 1980s, a situation that worsened in the following decade.

The constitutional revision of 1989, which emerged in the context of a liberalizing economic reform, dictated the inclusion of cooperatives in the third

---

[14] The cooperative code was later revised by the Law no. 51/96 of 7 September and altered by the Decree-Law no. 343/98 of 6 November (José António Rodrigues, 'O quadro jurídico', p. 127).
[15] Rodrigues, p. 127.
[16] Interviewed at his office in September 2013. The interview was taped with his consent.
[17] Namorado, 'Cooperativismo e política em Portugal', p. 110.

sector, together with associations, mutualities and foundations — the private initiatives of public utility that presently constitute the cooperative and social sector. This option reflected a change in the role attributed to cooperatives; if in the initial formulation of the Constitution they were understood as a cornerstone for the development of social property and an instigator of the transition to socialism, in 1989, under a majority Social Democratic Party (PSD) government, they became just another element in a mixed and stable economy. Socialism was no longer an option and capitalism was no longer just a stepping stone, it was the undisputed economic model adopted by Portuguese democracy.

As noted by Sebastián Royo and Paul Christopher Manuel,[18] Portuguese policy makers during the 1980s relied on accession to the EEC to assist in the consolidation of the recent democratic institutions, which implied a modernization of the economic structures and a normalization of the relations with the other member states in a context of instability of the institutions that had been established during the transition to democracy. The integration process entailed the promotion of economic competition, the privatization of public enterprises, the restructuring of the industrial sector, and a process of economic deregulation — measures that drove Portugal further away from the socialist path.

The Turning Point

The influence of the European Union (EU) in contemporary Portuguese political development is an explanatory factor to consider in the decline of the cooperative sector and to some extent can be viewed as a new critical juncture that somehow reversed the effects of the critical juncture that preceded it — the revolutionary transition to democracy. This phenomenon has not been felt in the associative movement, which has been thriving, but the cooperative movement, given its economic specificities, has been affected. The EU's neoliberal orientation, enforced particularly through the influence of the Thatcher governments, motivated member states to undertake processes of privatization and deregulation with the goal of intensifying market competition, thereby reducing the role of the state in the provision of services and expanding the role of the markets. This process, facilitated by the Single Market and by Economic and Monetary Union, implies that a more intense competition leads organizations to perform more efficiently,[19] an objective that is openly prioritized over cooperation.

As such, the socialist alternative proposed by the cooperative sector was

---

[18] Sebastián Royo and Paul Christopher Manuel, 'Reconsidering Economic Relations and Political Citizenship in the New Iberia of the New Europe: Some Lessons from the Fifteenth Anniversary of the Accession of Portugal and Spain to the European Union', *Centre for European Studies Working Paper*, 94 (2003).
[19] Peter Hall, 'Institutions and the Evolution of European Democracy', in *Governing Europe*, ed. by Jack Hayward and Anand Menon (Oxford: Oxford University Press, 2013), pp. 1–14.

removed to the backstage where, in the understanding of some of its actors, it longs for new opportunities. The manager of an umbrella organization operating in the cooperative sector considers that it is a strategic partner of the state that presents an alternative to capitalism, with its own jobs, agents and resources. In his own words:

> Capitalism is dying a slow death and other opportunities will come. The capitalist company is very recent and it is very difficult to ascertain who the agents are in the capitalist economy. Cooperatives will be one of the possible solutions for the future problems of human societies, privileging cooperation between individuals above individual profit.[20]

A report by the National Statistical Centre (INE) provides an exhaustive overview of the social and cooperative sector. This report on the Satellite Account of the Social Economy for the year 2010 presents the analysis, by type of activity, of all relevant entities.[21] According to the report, the Gross Value Added (GVA) of the social economy at that time represented 2.8% of the total national GVA and 5.5% of full-time paid employment. Out of the 55,383 organizations considered, associations and other similar social economy organizations, such as organizations of volunteer firefighters, were predominant and represented almost the totality of the sector — 94%, accounting for 54.1% of GVA (see Fig. 2). Cooperatives were the second largest group in terms of number of units (4%) and GVA (17%).[22]

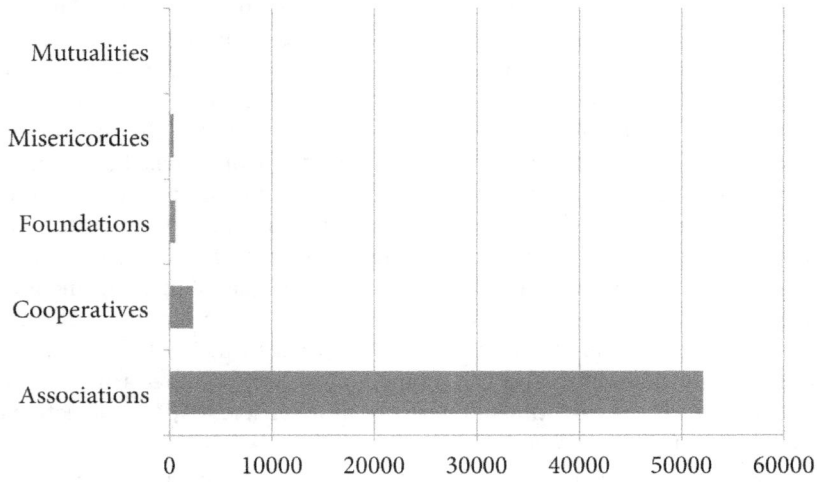

FIG. 2: Number of organizations in the social and cooperative sector by type, in 2010. Source: INE, 2013, p. 19.

[20] Interviewed at his office in September 2013. The interview was taped with his consent.
[21] *Conta Satélite da Economia Social 2010* (Lisbon: CASES, 2013).
[22] INE (2013), *Conta Satélite da Economia Social* (Lisbon: INE, 2013), pp. 5–6.

In 2010, there were 2260 registered cooperatives, with the largest group operating in the areas of trade, consumption and services (26.2%). Activities related to development, housing and the environment also presented a significant weight (17.8%). It is estimated that cooperatives had a financial surplus of approximately €170.3 million in 2010, and their resources were estimated at €2950.1 million. As for the structure of these resources, the report concluded that production is the main source of funding and that property income assumes a greater relative weight in cooperatives that have a financial activity (47.1%).[23]

The connotation of cooperatives with socialism seems to have hindered their development and minimized their relevance, as the policy towards the sector was often ambiguous and contradictory: although institutional bodies and constitutional measures were created and defined to protect the cooperative sector, the legislation did not always follow this tendency. For instance, in the mid-1980s, access to some economic areas was denied to the cooperative sector, including life insurance brokerage, transport of merchandise and vehicle rental.[24] The fiscal policy towards the sector has also not been favourable. A legal expert in the social and cooperative sector believes that cooperatives lost some fiscal advantages, and that the cooperative sector has been neglected by policy makers over recent years.[25] In agreement with this view, the manager of an umbrella organization operating in the cooperative sector considers that it has been weakened because the support that the movement had during and after the revolution was gradually lost for political reasons, and the constitutional requirements were no longer fulfilled.[26]

Cavaco Silva and the Cooperative Movement

The first signs of decline of the cooperative sector began in the early 1990s, during the Cavaco Silva governments,[27] which entailed profound structural reforms that broke with the revolution's socialist orientation. The main goal was to make the transition to a liberal economic system, based on private ownership, which would enable Portugal to align itself with its European partners, after becoming a member of the EEC in 1986. These reforms involved the privatization of public companies in key sectors of the economy or the concession of their management to private companies. Sectors such as telecommunications, transport and production were affected by such changes. Other measures included the reform of the agriculture sector, with a reinforcement of private

[23] INE, pp. 22–24.
[24] Namorado, 'Cooperativismo e política em Portugal'.
[25] Interviewed at his office in October 2013. The interview was taped with his consent.
[26] Interviewed at his office in September 2013. The interview was taped with his consent.
[27] Aníbal Cavaco Silva (Social Democratic Party — PSD) was elected prime minister for three consecutive terms: he held office in a minority government from 1985 to 1987 and in two majority governments from 1987 to 1991 and from 1991 to 1995.

property; the facilitation of the termination of employment contracts; the reduction of obstacles to the privatization and development of the financial system; and the revision of the fiscal system, particularly in the area of direct income taxation, with a simplification of regulations and procedures.

Cooperatives were not absent from the governments' projects. The programme of the 10th Constitutional Government (1985–87) stressed 'the importance of cooperative development and its contribution to the quality of life of the Portuguese people, achieved through greater social justice, an improvement of the production and marketing channels and an effective response to the needs of the people'.[28] The government aimed to support the cooperative sector and to assist it in meeting the challenges entailed in EEC membership. The programme of the 11th Constitutional Government (1987–91) maintained the support to the cooperative sector, which was viewed as an important instrument of 'social progress' and a key element in the 'reduction of tensions and conflicts'.[29] The plan was to consolidate the sector through awareness-raising actions, training programmes and technical support, particularly to cooperatives in branches that could give a greater contribution to socioeconomic development and job creation. The programme of the 12th Constitutional Government (1991–95) was coherent with its predecessors and continued to regard the cooperative sector as a source of 'civic education', a 'promoter of solidarity' and a valuable contributor to 'economic development' and 'social progress'.[30] Cooperative organization was considered 'very demanding' and it was deemed necessary 'to be very selective regarding the sectors where it can flourish'. The modernization and professionalization of the management bodies of cooperatives was understood as fundamental for their adaptation to European demands and competitiveness, which emerged as more relevant than the cooperative principles.

In spite of this apparent support to the cooperative sector, it is during the Cavaco Silva's majority governments that the formation of new cooperatives starts to show a decline, which suggests that political speech does not always translate into practice. Rui Namorado (op. cit.) saw here a hidden state agenda of obstructing cooperative development, an opinion shared by the manager of an umbrella organization operating in the cooperative sector, who confirmed that the loss of positive discrimination for the cooperative sector was particularly notable during the Cavaco Silva governments.[31]

---

[28] Programme of the 10th Constitutional Government, online at <https://www.historico.portugal.gov.pt/pt/o-governo/arquivo-historico/governos-constitucionais/gc10/programa-do-governo/programa-do-x-governo-constitucional.aspx>, p. 45.
[29] Programme of the 11th Constitutional Government, online at <https://www.historico.portugal.gov.pt/pt/o-governo/arquivo-historico/governos-constitucionais/gc11/programa-do-governo/programa-do-xi-governo-constitucional.aspx>.
[30] Programme of the 12th Constitutional Government, online at <https://www.historico.portugal.gov.pt/pt/o-governo/arquivo-historico/governos-constitucionais/gc12/programa-do-governo/programa-do-xii-governo-constitucional.aspx>.
[31] Interviewed at his office in September 2013. The interview was taped with his consent.

The Cooperative Movement in a Capitalist System

Gomes Santos identifies two models to characterize state–cooperative relations in Portugal: a 'developing model', implemented from 1980 to 1988, and a 'disadvantageous neutral model', implemented from 1989 to 1994.[32] The first model was characterized by fiscal benefits to cooperatives, which implied a generic immunity of cooperative activity from business taxation. The second model, initiated with the Tax Reform on Income and Real Estate (1989), was characterized by a mercantilist and profit-orientated approach to cooperative activity that understood cooperatives in the same way as any other commercial or industrial entity, and determined a reduction of the benefits formerly granted to the sector. This policy involved, among other measures, the disappearance of the generic exemption that covered all liquid surpluses generated by cooperatives; the exclusion of all cooperatives from the exemption of profit subjected to Corporation Tax (IRC — Imposto sobre o Rendimento de Pessoas Coletivas); and the restriction of exemptions provided to housing cooperatives.[33]

A third moment in the state–cooperative sector relation was also envisaged by Gomes Santos, a 'supportive strategic model', initiated in 1995 with the constitution of an inter-ministerial committee to redefine the fiscal policy for the cooperative sector and by a tax reform that included the adaptation of the tax regime for the social economy. However, the decline of the cooperative sector continued, with fewer cooperatives being constituted each year. This suggests that the policy measures adopted during the Cavaco Silva governments generated a path dependency that has not significantly altered since then.

According to the manager of an umbrella organization operating in the cooperative sector, the positive differentiation for the cooperative sector tends to be attenuated but the government can always argue that it still exists, thus defending itself from any accusation of unconstitutionality.[34] For example, the legislation for the social economy recently approved unanimously by the parliament is very favourable and is in tune with the constitution, stating clearly that the state has the obligation to support cooperatives and that there must be a fiscal differentiation for the sector. This differentiation exists but it has been fading gradually because specific legislation on fiscal benefits or on access to credit does not follow these requirements.

Without consistent support from the state, agricultural and production cooperatives lost ground owing to a strongly competitive environment and the

---

[32] Gomes Santos 'A fiscalidade do cooperativismo português: evolução no período 1974/1998', in *Cooperativismo, emprego e economia social*, ed. by Carlos Pestana Barros and J. C. Gomes Santos (Lisbon: Vulgata: 1999), pp. 137–68.
[33] Before these alterations, only income earned in transactions with third parties was excluded from the exemption (Decree-Law no. 737-A/74 of 23 December). According to the new IRC Code, only income directly related with the construction, sale, purchase, repair or remodelling of homes for housing of its members was exempt.
[34] Interviewed at his office in September 2013. The interview was taped with his consent.

decline of some economic activities, such as metalwork and textile production. As an alternative, cooperatives turned to education, culture or services, or to other areas that were less appealing to the market economy, such as social services. It is a cooperative sector directed towards the satisfaction of the needs of heterogeneous users, understood as clients, and not a mobilization of supportive members towards common goals: these are cooperatives of services and not cooperatives run by their members. In some areas such as consumption, cooperatives have been trying to face the competition of the large commercial areas by fusing with each other. Cardoso Pereira considers that the adaptation effort made by cooperatives to adjust themselves to a mass consumer society compromises their classist basis and their own identity.[35]

As stated by a legal expert in the social and cooperative sector, there is a mixture of capitalist interests with cooperative interests, a situation that intensified with adherence to the European Union and the strong economic competition it generated.[36] As a result, the frontier between cooperatives and for-profit companies is increasingly blurred: there are for-profit companies constituted by cooperatives, cooperatives constituted by companies and associations between small and medium sized companies, and cooperatives, constituted to face the competition of 'big capital'.

Housing Cooperatives

Cooperative construction reached its peak in 1989 with 4582 dwellings contracted, but after that that it has been decreasing dramatically.[37] During and immediately after the revolution, cooperatives were seen as a valuable instrument in meeting the severe housing needs that affected the country. In the late 1970s, the cooperative movement was responsible for the development of residential complexes which were innovative in their user-involvement approach. These projects presented high quality standards, outdoor spaces and social facilities, something which was unprecedented in housing built at controlled costs in Portugal. The extinction of the Housing Support Fund (FFH — Fundo de Fomento à Habitação) in the early 1980s temporarily disturbed the ongoing cooperative processes, but the creation of the National Housing Institute (INH) favoured a new phase of development.

At the end of the 1980s, a government plan to promote housing at controlled costs raised hopes that were frustrated by unfavourable policy measures and by the absence of an effective dialogue between the government and the social partners in the construction sector. As a consequence, housing cooperatives began to experience difficulties in the development of their projects, particularly those directed towards the most disadvantaged social groups. As such, the 1990s

---

[35] Cardoso Pereira, *Associativismo e capital social*.
[36] Interviewed at his office in October 2013. The interview was taped with his consent.
[37] IHRU, *Relatório 2 — Políticas de habitação* (Lisbon: ISCTE, IRIC/UP, 2007), p. 26.

represented a period of withdrawal of the prior expectations of consolidation and growth.

The state itself has been withdrawing from housing construction, understood as an unwelcomed expense that should be left in the hands of the market.[38] And the market did take over, as is clearly shown in the following graphic: the houses and flats completed from 1997 to 2012 were mostly built through private initiative. Housing construction reached its peak in 2002 with the completion of 129,278 units, 124,864 (96.5%) of which were of private initiative, 2555 (2%) of public initiative and 1859 (1.5%) of cooperative initiative. From then on the crisis in construction led to a constant decrease in the number of dwellings completed each year, which reached its bottom in 2012 with just 34,294 units (see Fig. 3). The crisis transversely affected all sectors — private, public and cooperative, which in that year finished, respectively, only 33,703 (98.3%), 507 (1.5%) and 84 (0.2%) units, but the relative weight of both the public and the cooperative sectors decreased even more in comparison with 2002.

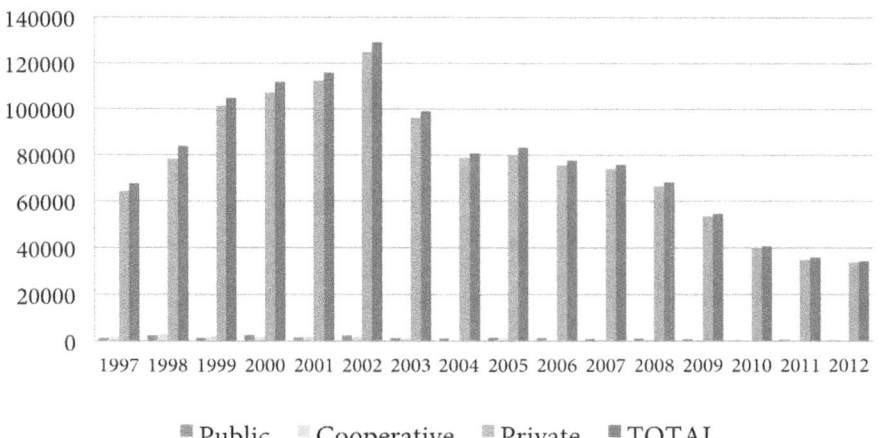

■ Public   Cooperative   ■ Private   ■ TOTAL

FIG. 3: Number of dwellings completed by sector, 1997 to 2012
Source: INE, 2013, p. 31.

Housing cooperatives have been faced with several difficulties that hinder their competitiveness. The cooperative tax status, define by the Law no. 85/98, of 16 December 1998, opened the possibility for cooperatives to use non-subsidized loans for construction of housing within controlled cost parameters (though these were increased by 20%), the application of reduced

---

[38] Marina Carreiras, Bárbara Ferreira, Anselmo Amílcar and Jorge Malheiros, 'Notas sobre a situação da habitação social em Portugal: geografia, problemas e oportunidades?', *VIII Congresso da geografia portuguesa: repensar a geografia para novos desafios* (Lisbon: Associação Portuguesa de Geógrafos, 2011).

Value Added Tax (VAT) rates, and other tax benefits, such as the exemption from the Municipal Tax on Real Estate Transfer (IMT) in land acquisition and the Municipal Tax on Real Estate (IMI) in the case of residential buildings of urban collective property destined for the members of the cooperatives. In metropolitan areas, the use of this statute facilitated the construction of better-quality housing priced below the free market.[39] Decree-Law no. 145/97, of 11 July 1997, stipulated that housing cooperatives have the right to several advantages, such as subsidized loans for construction; a reduction in VAT in construction at controlled costs; the exemption from IMT for the acquisition of construction land; exemption from the payment of fees and charges for the construction of urban infrastructures and of registration fees and charges related to mortgage loans; and registration acts made free of charge.

However, the Institute for Housing and Urban Rehabilitation (IHRU — Instituto da Habitação e da Reabilitação Urbana) found several shortcomings related to a disconnection between the construction costs and sale values of the houses, in light of the requirements for construction, in particular those concerning: accessibility and the heating requirements of buildings; the absence of any limitation or requirement on the household as to who could access this type of housing; the preference for individual ownership of the houses; the preference for acquisition instead of renting; and a production capacity constrained by the scarcity of land compatible with the promotion of housing at controlled costs.

The problem of access to affordable construction land is one of the main constraints, considering the lack of differentiated financial mechanisms for reimbursement of the costs. The lack of land for construction in the most central city areas compels cooperatives to look for it on the outskirts, which entails additional travel costs for potential members. The progressive territorial expansion of Municipal Master Plans (MDPs) made it difficult for municipalities to acquire land at low prices and pass it on to cooperatives, since the regulated zoning of urban land raised the expectations of the owners regarding the value of their land. The absence of a special regime of expropriation for cooperative development aggravated this situation since it favoured a pricing of expropriation at current market value.

This situation prevented the city councils from building up a reserve of municipal land that could support cooperative construction for non-solvent social strata. Finally, the benefits granted by IHRU to housing construction at controlled costs (subsidizing a third of the current interest rate) did not compensate for the excessive bureaucracy involved in the approval of the projects.[40] The officer responsible for the cooperative sector in one city council declared that the bureaucracy is such that an allotment process may take up to 12 years: 'frequently, when the City Council believes the process of allocation is

---

[39] IHRU, p. 78.
[40] IHRU, pp. 74–77.

concluded, the Land Registry considers that there were shortcomings in certain aspects that have to be revised, and so the process has to be started again from square one'.[41]

On top of all these constraints on cooperative development, Bingre do Amaral mentions the gradual transformation of housing into a financial asset detached from its real purpose,[42] a phenomenon that has been supported by urban planning legislation that favours the private ownership of land as an economic factor, relegating its social function to the background.[43] The system of spatial planning determines which land will absorb, through its price, the availability of mortgage credit and, consequently, which entities will benefit from the future rents entailed in these mortgages. As Fig. 3 showed, these entities were not housing cooperatives, but the construction companies and the banks.

Despite some attempts to liberalize and modernize the rental market, the stimulation was very weak and the outright acquisition of a house maintained its dominance in the housing market.[44] This situation was facilitated by low tax rates, subsidized credit schemes and favourable loan legislation, which artificially increased the purchasing power of the Portuguese population.

When it became a member of the EEC, Portugal's determination of exchange rates had to take into account its integration into Economic and Monetary Union. This meant that the deficit of the public sector could not exceed 3% of GDP, the public sector debt could not exceed 60% of GNP, the inflation rate could only be 1% above the average of the three best rates in the EEC and the stability of the exchange rate had to be maintained within the European Monetary System. Consequently, there was a decline in interest rates, which greatly facilitated access to credit.[45] The volume of mortgage credits increased from 5000 million euros in 1990 to 104,000 million euros in 2008, and in this year about 68% of the private Portuguese debt resulted from these mortgages.[46]

Easy access to credit made the housing market more dependent on interest rates than on demographic pressure or on the real income of the Portuguese population. Moreover, a favourable fiscal policy promoted the retention of houses, including vacant ones, for speculation, thus artificially lowering the supply and turning it into the 'good and safe investment' for everyone. The officer responsible for the cooperative sector in one city council considers that

---

[41] Interviewed at her office in April 2013. The interview was taped with her consent.
[42] Pedro Bingre do Amaral, *Análise das relações da política de solos com o sistema económico: estudo de enquadramento para a preparação da Nova Lei do Solo* (Lisbon: Ministério do Ambiente e do Ordenamento do Território — Direção-Geral do Ordenamento do Território e do Desenvolvimento Urbano, 2011), p. 15.
[43] See for example Decree-Law no. 46 673/65 of 29 November on the juridical regime of urban allocations, whose spirit is still present in recent legislation, or the Decree-Law no. 168/99 of 18 May, which approved the code of expropriations.
[44] Rui Paulo Figueiredo, *Aníbal Cavaco Silva e o PSD (1985–1995): a pós-consolidação do regime democrático português* (Lisbon: Hugin Editores, 2004).
[45] Figueiredo, p. 272.
[46] Bingre do Amaral.

the need to own things, including houses, was inculcated in the Portuguese citizens through the aggressive credit advertising conducted by financial institutions. Cooperatives were caught in this process and became detached from their initial goal:

> In these new cooperatives, the members rapidly become proprietors of their house, once it is built, and immediately detach themselves from the cooperative. The spirit of ownership constantly overshadows the spirit of cooperation. Currently, I would say that what makes people join a cooperative is not the spirit of cooperation but this need that has arisen which requires that a person must be the owner of a house.[47]

This led to another problem: an excess of houses in the market. From a dramatic shortage of adequate households, Portugal evolved to an excess of available housing and it presents the second highest ratio in the EU of dwellings per family (1.5), after Spain.[48] In the last three decades, housing provision has grown considerably, as did the average comfort levels of the dwellings. About 18% of the buildings were built after 1960 and 30% were built during the last two decades.[49] However, the growth in numbers did not signify an end to ongoing problems nor did it prevent the emergence of new ones, such as overcrowding, household insolvency and indebtedness, lack of adequate bathing facilities and other housing amenities, and an increase in the number of senior citizens living alone. The deterioration of older buildings is also a continuing problem, particularly in the historic centres of major cities and, considering the poor quality of recent construction, this problem is expected to intensify in the future and to be exacerbated by the economic crisis, which will make it difficult for the owners to carry out the maintenance of their houses.

One can also observe a significant increase in the number of houses that are repossessed by the banks because the owners cannot repay their loans. In the early stages of the crisis, in 2009, there were 127,377 people in a situation of mortgage default, but by 2013 the number had increased to 145,766.[50] The economic crisis dictated a decrease in the purchasing power that affected most of the population, including the middle class, a situation worsened by an inversion of the credit policy of the banks, which began to adopt much more restrictive measures. This behaviour was due, firstly, to an increase in the cost of capital, which made it difficult for banks to finance themselves and, secondly, to the sharp deterioration of expectations regarding economic activity in general and the housing market in particular, which included a decrease in the banks' expectations as to the capacity of consumers to meet their mortgage responsibilities.

---

[47] Interviewed at her office in October 2013. The interview was taped with her consent.
[48] Bingre do Amaral, p. 34, quoting INE.
[49] Teresa Sá Marques, Fátima Loureiro Matos, Paula Guerra and Diogo Ribeiro, 'Housing Problems in Portugal: A Challenge to Define a Territorialised Policy in Times of Crisis', in *The Welfare State in Portugal in the Age of Austerity* (Lisbon: ISEG, 2014), p. 2.
[50] Sá Marques et al., p. 12, quoting the Bank of Portugal.

As a result, the low to average income citizen could no longer afford to buy a house, either through cooperative initiative or in the free market. It also takes much more time to sell a house than it did a few years ago: in 2006, the average time to sell a house in Portugal was eight months, but in 2013 it had more than doubled, to seventeen months.[51] A legal expert in the social and cooperative sector describes the strong negative impact this situation had in the housing cooperative sector:

> Housing cooperatives have been suffering a lot with the crisis in construction. Because of this, many are now bankrupt. The new credit lines that were created for the cooperative sector are insignificant, compared with their needs, and their effects are not felt. These are loans that need to be repaid and so housing cooperatives don't even apply because they cannot pay. There is no market for their offer, so they have no resources.[52]

The strain put on housing cooperatives had its consequences. In 2008, three new housing cooperatives were set up, while twelve were closed down, making it the worst ratio of the various cooperative branches, although the housing sector still remained the second most significant (17%), after the agricultural branch (27.4%).[53] In 2009, there were eight housing cooperatives in the ranking of the 100 largest cooperatives in Portugal, with the largest of these, the Urbanização Varandas de Queijas (CUPH), occupying 42nd place.[54]

Conclusion

Housing cooperatives in Portugal are faced with the urgent need to reinvent themselves and rethink their purpose, since the product they traditionally offer is now in surplus. They can direct themselves towards rebuilding, urban requalification, rental or the management of urban areas, but this adaptation remains to be made, because it requires funding. The officer responsible for the cooperative sector in a city council confirms that the city council has cooperation protocols with some cooperatives that manage municipal neighbourhoods, but considers that housing cooperatives have no money to invest in urban rehabilitation due to their financial difficulties.[55] Many of their members are demanding that the money they have invested be refunded.

Even if they want to sell the land they already acquired, they cannot, at least not for the same acquisition prices. Many are now bankrupt. In the face of all these difficulties and in an effort to become more competitive, housing cooperatives have tended to adopt the business management models of construction companies and so run the risk of deviating from their founding

---

[51] Sá Marques et al., p. 14, quoting Confidencial Imobiliário/ PORDATA.
[52] Interviewed at his office in October 2013. The interview was taped with his consent.
[53] INSCOOP, *Anuário comercial do sector cooperative, 2009/2010* (Lisbon: INSCOOP, 2010), pp. 5-6.
[54] CASES, *As 100 maiores empresas cooperativas* (Lisbon: CASES, 2011), pp. 34-40.
[55] Interviewed at her office in October 2013. The interview was taped with her consent.

principles and leaving behind people with a lower income. They may opt for a middle and upper-middle class that can afford to access the free market, thereby undermining their status of public utility and their role as instruments of social policy.[56]

The data suggests that cooperatives lack the autonomy generally enjoyed by associations. Their dependency on the state and the market constrains their capacity to act according to their principles and, more than that, it hinders their activity. The decline of housing cooperatives in democratic Portugal can be partially explained by the economic vocation of the cooperative sector, which leads it to compete with the corporate sector in a context of market capitalism that privileges profit. Their competitive disadvantage puts cooperatives into a situation of dependency on the regulatory instruments of the state, which has proved unwilling to promote any consistently positive discrimination for the sector, as it has valued competitiveness and economic growth over cooperation and solidarity.

Housing cooperatives have reacted to this by trying to compete with construction companies in a territory that is not their own — the territory of growth and profit, not the territory of cooperation and public service. In attempting to do this, they tend to adjust their management models and seek out more solvent members. To make things worse, citizens are often ill-informed about the cooperative sector, are oriented towards profit, and are mainly motivated by private ownership.

As such, their desire to participate leads them to seek forms of involvement that require smaller financial risk, such as through associations, which have been decidedly successful in the period since 1974, as their growth and density clearly demonstrates. The egalitarian transition to democracy in Portugal made it easy for associations to become embedded in the newly created regulation and policy-making networks without giving up their autonomy, and to the present day they remain fundamental actors in Portuguese democracy.

Cooperatives, as we have seen, face greater difficulties. A professional in the social and cooperative sector declared that one of the greatest challenges for the sector is to inform the general population, particularly the younger generation, since it is virtually unknown and it is thought to depend solely on voluntarism, without professionalization; it is often associated with the 'traditional wine cellar where the grandfather trades his grapes or potatoes'.[57]

Business degrees, particularly in the most renowned universities where the leading Portuguese managers and administrators are trained, often do not cover the cooperative sector. These students are hard to reach, since the 'not-for-profit concept is particularly difficult to grasp in a context where the main goal is to work for a multinational company and earn a lot of money'.[58] As a

---

[56] IHRU.
[57] Interviewed at her office in October 2013. The interview was taped with her consent.
[58] Ibid.

result, the future of the cooperative sector in Portugal is uncertain, because it tends to play a marginal role in key sectors of the economy or to be left to less competitive areas. Housing construction is definitely not one of these spare market niches.

The Portuguese Presidencies of the European Union: A Preliminary Study

NUNO SEVERIANO TEIXEIRA AND
REINALDO SARAIVA HERMENEGILDO

*Instituto Português de Relações Internacionais (IPRI-NOVA)/
Academia Militar and IPRI-NOVA*

Introduction

The Presidency of the European Union or, more precisely, the Rotating Presidency of the Council of Ministers of the European Union, is a key institution in the European process both for the Union and its Member States.

The Treaty of Lisbon introduced, in this domain, a number of significant changes, and created a dual presidency system — at once supranational, at the level of the European Council and the General Affairs and External Relations Council, and intergovernmental, at the level of the sectorial councils, in which it preserved the rotating presidency. As such, the rotating presidency of the Council of Ministers retains a relevant role.[1]

At a European level, the presidency is regarded by the other actors as the European leadership, and is expected not only to manage the present but, more important still, to know how to plan for the future. At member state level, holding the presidency is regarded not only as an opportunity to lead the Union, but also as a chance to bring national interests into the European agenda and to influence the future of Europe. Granted, the levels of influence are different according to different presidencies,[2] but if this is true as a general principle, it is also true a fortiori in the case of small member states that have a limited weight in the context of the Union and regard the presidency as a unique opportunity to increase it, at least for six months.[3]

---

[1] See Treaty on European Union, article 16, no. 9; Treaty on the Functioning of the European Union, article 236, (b), no. 9, in *Tratado de Lisboa anotado e comentado*, ed. by Manuel Lopes Porto and Gonçalo Anastácio (Lisbon: Almedina, 2012); and the decision of the Council of 1 December 2009, establishing the measures deriving from the European Council's decision concerning the exercise of the presidency of the Council preparatory bodies, see Conselho Europeu, 'Decisão relativa à Presidência do Conselho' (2009/881/UE), *Jornal Oficial da União Europeia*, 1 December 2009. Conselho Europeu, Bruxelas, 9 December 2009.

[2] Simone Bunse, *Small States and EU Governance: Leadership through the Council Presidency* (Oxford: Palgrave Macmillan, 2009).

[3] Reinaldo Saraiva Hermenegildo, *As Presidências portuguesas da União Europeia* (Porto: Fronteira do Caos, 2017).

The functions of the presidency are not formally laid down in the Treaties, but rather they have evolved and been consolidated by established practice throughout the process of European integration.[4] Today they are essentially four: organization, management and coordination of the works of the Council; agenda-setting and definition of political priorities; mediation in negotiating and decision-making processes; and, finally, representation, both internal, in relation to other European institutions, and external, in the international framework.[5]

Despite the common functional framework of presidencies, the exercise of these functions leaves a fair amount of leeway for the member states and, consequently, each presidency is different: more low profile or high profile; more or less successful; with a more or less pronounced administrative or political character. For member states, particularly small states, the presidency is thus a window of opportunity that allows them to combine formal and informal powers, obtaining in this fashion, albeit temporarily, a comparative advantage in relation to other EU member states and institutions. However, the characteristics and the degree of success of the presidency will depend not only on these factors but also on defined political priorities and on the level of proficiency of the exercise, as the presidency does not act in a *vacuum*.[6]

Portugal has held the presidency of the European Union on three occasions: in the first semester of 1992, in the first semester of 2000, and in the second semester of 2007. And along the way, the exercise of Portuguese presidencies evolved from a presidency with an administrative character and internal priorities, in 1992, to presidencies with political concerns and European priorities, in 2000 and 2007. The purpose of this paper is twofold: in the first place, to analyse, through a comparative perspective, the three historical cases of the Portuguese presidencies of the EU and to identify a pattern of national behaviour; and secondly, to determine a theoretical reading of the Portuguese presidencies, taking as a starting point the proposal of Elgström and Tallberg, namely the two explanatory logics underlying two different approaches — the rational approach and the sociological approach.[7]

---

[4] Jonas Tallberg, *Responsabilité sans Pouvoir? The Agenda-Shaping Powers of the EU Council Presidency*, (2001) <http://www.svet.lu.se/projekt/presidency/agendashaping.pdf> [accessed 5 April 2012]. See also: Helen Wallace, 'The Presidency of the Council of Ministers of the European Community: Tasks and Evolution', in *The Presidency of the European Council of Ministers: Impacts and Implications for National Governments*, ed. by C. O'Nuallain (London: Croom Helm, 1985), pp. 1–21; Emil Joseph Kirchner, *Decision Making in the European Community: The Council Presidency and European Integration* (Manchester: Manchester University Press, 1992); Adriaan Schout, 'The Presidency as Juggler: Managing Conflicting Expectations', *EIPASCOPE*, 2 (1998), 1–9 <http://aei.pitt.edu/785/1/scop98_2_1.pdf> [accessed 22 July 2013]; Reinaldo Saraiva Hermenegildo, pp. 87–130.
[5] Ole Elgström, 'Introduction', in *European Union Council Presidencies: A Comparative Perspective*, ed. by Ole Elgström (London: Routledge, 2003), pp. 1–17 (pp. 4–6).
[6] Simone Bunse, p. 73.
[7] Ole Elgström and Jonas Tallberg, 'Conclusion: Rationalist and Sociological Perspectives on the Council Presidency', in *European Union Council Presidencies: A Comparative Perspective*, ed. by Ole Elgström (London: Routledge, 2003), pp. 191–205.

A Theoretical Framework for the EU Presidencies

Theoretical literature devoted to the study of the Presidencies of the Council of the European Union divides its analysis into two broad approaches: the rationalist approach and the sociological approach. These two streams present different perspectives, sometimes competing but, in fact, quite complementary. Based on studies of empirical cases of the performance of EU presidencies, they both rely on new approaches that give rise to a new debate: on the one hand, strategic behaviour, and on the other, roles and identity.[8] The rationalist approach focuses on the actors' rational efforts to reach their goals, while the sociological approach emphasizes the actors' roles and self-images. According to Elgström and Tallberg, the result of these two streams confirms how the rational and the ideational are interacting factors involved in the production of EU policies.[9]

The rationalist approach

In the rationalist perspective, power lies essentially with, and varies according to, the size and economic weight of each country. Hence, when large member states hold the presidency, given the resources available to them, they have, to start with, an increased capacity and a greater influence in the performance of their duties.[10] According to the rationalist perspective, the choice of negotiation strategies is the product of a strategic configuration combining a variety of factors: concerns about reputation; distribution of preferences; decision-making and legislative procedure rules.[11] In this respect, it is regarded as a governance policy based on a 'logic of expected consequences'.[12] And, to that extent, the choices involved in this approach to the presidency concern EU negotiations and decision-making in a strategic environment, in which the actors, including the presidency, are rational, and which endeavours to achieve, in a largely exogenous manner, a number of priorities. The presidency is conceived as a cost-benefit relationship and, for the presidency-in-office, it constitutes an opportunity to defend its own national interests.[13]

In Tallberg's view,[14] the presidency encompasses a vast set of power resources

---

[8] Ole Elgström and Jonas Tallberg, p. 191.
[9] Ole Elgström and Jonas Tallberg, p. 191.
[10] Lucia Quaglia and Edward Moxon-Browne, 'What makes a good EU Presidency? Italy and Ireland Compared', *Journal of Common Market Studies*, 44.2 (2006), 349–68.
[11] Ole Elgström and Jonas Tallberg, p. 198.
[12] James G. March and Johan P. Olsen, 'The Institutional Dynamics of International Political Orders', *International Organization*, 52.4 (1998), 943–69 (pp. 949–50).
[13] Ole Elgström and Jonas Tallberg, pp. 191–205.
[14] Jonas Tallberg, 'The Agenda-Shaping Powers of the EU Council Presidency', *Journal of European Public Policy*, 10.1 (2003), 1–19; Jonas Tallberg, 'The Power of the Presidency: Brokerage, Efficiency and Distribution in EU Negotiations', *Journal of Common Market Studies*, 5 (2004), 999–1022; Jonas Tallberg, *Leadership and Negotiation in the European Union* (Cambridge: Cambridge University Press, 2006).

that enable the member state to promote its own priorities during its office. Above all, presidencies are endowed with a range of informational powers, given the privileged access to information, and of significant procedural powers, owing to asymmetrical control over negotiation procedures.

According to rationalist theory, no presidency adopts exclusively one or the other strategy conditioned solely by what is expected of it, but rather it adapts its negotiation strategy to the specific situations at hand. One typically ideal situation is the 'forcing' strategy — in other words, when national interests are at stake, reputational concerns are secondary, and the distribution of preferences is such that goals can only be reached by exploring all the means at the presidency's disposal.[15] Another ideal-typical situation is the 'accommodating' strategy. That is to say, when the presidency has only secondary interests at stake, reputational concerns are of great importance and an agreement can only be reached if the presidency sacrifices its own major concerns. However, the problem-solving strategy, in which the presidency seeks to maximize joint gains, is the most common strategy.[16]

Yet, there are also institutional constraints,[17] and the presidency's behaviour is not always characterized by 'forcing' strategies, with a view only to maximizing its individual interests, or 'competitive strategies', with the goal of achieving relative advantages. It can also be characterized by 'accommodating' strategies, essentially focused on the maximization of other parties' interests as, for example, when the presidency needs to prove its 'European credentials'.[18] However, the rationalist approach does not attach too great an importance to institutions[19] and states play the most important role, while their presidencies pursue mainly their own national interests.

Furthermore, when norms are observed, they are as a result of cost-benefit calculations, as non-compliance could compromise their reputation, elicit an uncooperative attitude from other states, or create a precedent for subsequent presidencies.[20] This is especially the case in the fields of management, external representation and political leadership duties. The role of mediator can be facilitated by the presidency's available resources, in the case of large countries, to change the position of reluctant States.[21] This perspective focuses, therefore, on the actors' conscious and rational efforts to reach their goals.[22]

Interaction between member states and institutions is regarded as an additional tool for member states to pursue and assure their national interests.

---

[15] Ole Elgström and Jonas Tallberg, p. 198.
[16] Ole Elgström and Jonas Tallberg, p. 198.
[17] Ole Elgström and Jonas Tallberg, pp. 192 and 196.
[18] Ole Elgström, p. 12.
[19] Jonas Tallberg, *Leadership and Negotiation*, p. 5.
[20] Arne Niemann and Jeannette Mak, '(How) do norms guide Presidency behaviour in EU negotiations?', *Working Paper* (Dublin: UCD Dublin European Institute), 09-10 (2009), 1–26 <https://www.ucd.ie/t4cms/WP_09-10_Niemann_and_Mak.pdf> [accessed 7 September 2017].
[21] Lucia Quaglia and Edward Moxon-Browne, pp. 349–68.
[22] Ole Elgström and Jonas Tallberg, p. 191.

In the Portuguese case the clearest example was interaction between the Commission and the Portuguese Presidency which led to the adoption of the Treaty of Lisbon. The office of the Presidency of the Council of the EU therefore creates opportunities in comparison with the exercise of other presidencies, in other contexts or international organizations.[23] According to this approach, the EU's decision-making process develops in a strategic context in which, rationally, governments and institutions interact to pursue their interests in an exogenous environment. Governments use the presidency's office as an additional means to ensure their national interests. And the formal and informal institutions — norms, decision-making rules, legislative procedures — activate and restrain the presidency in its behavioural choices, and in its interaction with other member states and institutions.[24]

In brief, the presidency is a window of opportunity for member states to shape the agenda of the EU, through the combination of institutional powers, formal and informal, that enable them to gain competitive advantage vis-à-vis other member states and European institutions, during their office, in the sense that they may influence agenda-setting.[25]

According to Elgström and Tallberg,[26] the rationalist approach to the EU's presidency encompasses three components:

(1) The formulation of the presidency's preferences and priorities by the aggregation of the national level;
(2) The impact of empowerment and limitation of domestic policy(ies) in the presidency's behaviour;
(3) The strategic interaction with other EU actors which is shaped by formal and informal constraints at a European level.

The variations among presidencies are explained by modifications between these key components of the strategic environment.[27]

The sociological approach

The sociological approach focuses on socially constructed factors such as the ideas of persuasion, knowledge, diplomatic skills, past experience with EU presidencies, foreign policy orientation and credibility of the President-in-office.[28] There are a number of streams, including constructivism, which conceptualize the interaction between member states in the EU based on non-material elements, meaning that there are forms of influence from the states other than material factors, such as economic and political weight and dimensions.[29]

[23] Ole Elgström and Jonas Tallberg, p. 192.
[24] Ole Elgström and Jonas Tallberg, p. 192.
[25] Simone Bunse, p. 71.
[26] Ole Elgström and Jonas Tallberg, p. 192.
[27] Ole Elgström and Jonas Tallberg, p. 192.
[28] Lucia Quaglia and Edward Moxon-Browne, pp. 349–68.
[29] Lucia Quaglia and Edward Moxon-Browne, pp. 349–68.

Contrary to the rationalist approach, according to the sociological approach the behaviour of the presidency is not guided by a 'logic of expected consequences'. The presidencies act and behave as they believe they must.[30] And the states holding the presidency comply with and respect the norm of neutrality and are impartial in the exercise of their functions. Thus, according to the sociological approach, governance hinges on policies based on a 'logic of appropriateness'. The actors' behaviour is determined by what they consider other actors' expectations of them to be, or by their own convictions — this means, the convictions they consider appropriate in a certain situation, not based on cost-benefit calculations.[31]

This approach stresses, therefore, the importance of norms and the role of ideas as explanatory variables of the presidency's behaviour. Equally relevant are each country's traditions, and the expectations and conceptions of roles played (and repeated) based on the member states' experience of previous presidencies. Collective expectations are also strongly determinant of what is considered appropriate behaviour.[32]

From the sociological perspective, the success of the presidency relies ultimately on non-material factors such as social acceptance, legitimacy and trust, and not on material factors such as economic and political weight and their hierarchy and real power.[33] In this context, it highlights the actors' roles and self-images,[34] or, in other words, their identities, based on national culture and historical traditions. These identities help to identify what roles presidencies prefer to play and how they prefer to fulfil these roles.[35]

Rationalist and sociological approaches: competing or complementary?

These two seemingly contradictory approaches can be, and often are, complementary. The sociological perspective addresses perceptions and identities, which shape the presidency's priorities. The rationalist perspective, on the other hand, concentrates on goals and means.[36] According to the former, the actors' performance relies essentially on past mechanisms related to the country's self-image and the traditional conception of their roles, which condition the definition of priorities and the options of certain policies. In the rationalist view, in contrast, the actor's performance ensues from the rational formulation of their national interests.[37] On the other hand, the sociological approach also emphasizes the impact of constitutional practices and the long-term international roles, shaped not only by geographical location but also by

[30] Ole Elgström and Jonas Tallberg, p. 198.
[31] James G. March and Johan P. Olsen, pp. 951–52.
[32] Arne Niemann and Jeannette Mak, p. 10.
[33] Arne Niemann and Jeannette Mak, p. 10. See also P. Terrence Hopmann, *The Negotiation Process and the Resolution of International Conflicts* (Columbia: University of South Carolina Press, 1996).
[34] Ole Elgström and Jonas Tallberg, p. 191.
[35] Ole Elgström and Jonas Tallberg, p. 198.
[36] Ole Elgström and Jonas Tallberg, p. 203.
[37] Ole Elgström and Jonas Tallberg, p. 203.

each country's specific historical experiences. For the rationalist approach, geographical location and the resources it provides are determinant for the definition of national interests.[38]

The sociological approach bases its explanatory logic on non-material factors and long-term trends. That is, the continuity of the states' behaviour is accounted for, essentially, in their relation to the permanence and persistence of images and national identities and the roles which they shape.[39] The rationalist approach, on the other hand, grounds its explanatory logic in material factors and short-term variations. The oscillation of the behaviour of states is explained essentially by the shifting of power relations in domestic politics.[40] The two approaches diverge at this point, but that is precisely why they are complementary. The former serves to account for the long-term — continuity in the performances of the presidencies; the latter, to account for the short-term — fluctuations in the strategic behaviour of the presidencies.[41]

Regarding reputation, the rationalist claim stresses the strategic value of a positive reputation, whereas the sociological claim underlines that a state must meet the expectations of others and behave appropriately.[42] Here, once again, the two approaches differ: for the rationalists, reputation is a goal insofar as it yields benefits, while for the sociological approach, it is the outcome of appropriate behaviour.

Finally, as regards compliance with the norm: according to the sociological perspective, presidencies follow the norm (of impartiality), since they internalize the values expressed by the norm itself, that can be viewed as a warranty. From the rationalist perspective, on the contrary, the presidency's conduct is based on cost-benefit analysis and, for that reason, states follow norms when benefits exceed costs. In both cases, the outcome may be the same, that is, there is compliance with the norm, yet for different reasons.[43]

From an empirical viewpoint, it is not possible to ascertain which approach is the most useful. What matters is that, theoretically, both have explanatory value. They are competing but, simultaneously, complementary. Furthermore, the competition and complementarity of the two perspectives creates a theoretical interaction that might contribute to a more thorough explanation of the behaviour of the presidencies.[44] It is, therefore, by means of that interaction that we seek a framework of analyses for the three Portuguese EU presidencies. And according to the theoretical framework presented here, both approaches are useful for explaining Portugal's behaviour and performance during its first presidency.

---

[38] Ole Elgström and Jonas Tallberg, p. 203.
[39] Ole Elgström and Jonas Tallberg, p. 203.
[40] Ole Elgström and Jonas Tallberg, pp. 203-04.
[41] Ole Elgström and Jonas Tallberg, p. 204.
[42] Ole Elgström and Jonas Tallberg, p. 204.
[43] Ole Elgström and Jonas Tallberg, p. 204.
[44] Ole Elgström and Jonas Tallberg, p. 204.

The Portuguese Presidencies of the EU Council

The first Portuguese presidency (1992)

The first years of Portugal's European integration, between 1986 and 1992, were marked by a political stance of caution and pragmatism and a European strategy oriented towards two main goals: the international credibility of full Portuguese membership and, simultaneously, seeking all the social and economic benefits arising from EEC integration.[45]

The first Portuguese presidency of the EU marked a decisive change in the process of Portugal's European integration.[46] In 1992, Portugal's position was still centred on economic and social issues, and was more cautious on a political level. It was determined more by the internal advantages that Portugal could enjoy from its presence in Europe than by any considered Portuguese perspective on the major European questions. Accordingly, the first presidency was focused on economic and social matters, and only the need to manage the Western Balkans situation, and the Danish rejection of the Maastricht Treaty, gave it any political dimension.

For Portuguese foreign policy, the first EU presidency was an 'absolute priority',[47] and it put to the test Portugal's level of European integration, and its capacity to lead the future of Europe. Besides the opportunity to influence the process of European integration, the presidency represented a unique chance, until then unprecedented, to affirm the country's international credibility at a European level. Portugal's main goal was not so much that of presenting new initiatives or a 'great vision' for Europe as of demonstrating its full integration in Europe and its capacity to organize and coordinate a European presidency.[48]

The priorities of the Portuguese presidency were of an essentially economic and social nature, with direct implications for domestic policy, especially in respect of the modernization of the country. This is the logic that explains the priority given to matters related to the Common Agricultural Policy (CAP), to social and economic cohesion, and to the Delors II Package, such as the Internal Market.[49] The majority of institutional and political questions that Portugal had to face — and even those concerning foreign policy (at the time, European Political Cooperation) — were inherited from previous presidencies

---

[45] Nuno Severiano Teixeira, 'Introduction: Portugal and European Integration, 1974–2010', in *The Europeanization of Portuguese Democracy*, ed. by Nuno Severiano Teixeira and António Costa Pinto (New York: Columbia University Press, 2012), p. 17.

[46] During this period, Aníbal Cavaco Silva was head of the Portuguese Government, with João de Deus Pinheiro as Foreign Minister and Vítor Martins was Secretary of State for European Integration.

[47] Ministério dos Negócios Estrangeiros, *Preparação da Primeira Presidência Portuguesa do Conselho das Comunidades Europeias* (Lisbon: MNE, 1988), p. 2.

[48] Ministério dos Negócios Estrangeiros, *Preparação da Primeira Presidência Portuguesa*, p. 3.

[49] Ministério dos Negócios Estrangeiros, *Portugal 92 — Presidência Portuguesa do Primeiro Semestre de 1992 — Rumo à União Europeia* (Lisbon: MNE, 1991), pp. 10–15.

or appeared on the agenda of the Portuguese presidency due to the situation in Europe,[50] as was the case with the EU Treaty negotiations.

On the other hand, the foreign policy priorities were not given significant emphasis by the Portuguese presidency, even those in which it became involved, such as the organization of the UN Conference on Environment and Development in Rio, the Uruguay Round, the solidarity programmes with Eastern Europe and the former Soviet Union, the third generation Agreement with Brazil, the support given to Southern Africa (mainly to Angola), and the first ministerial EEC–Mercosul meeting. These were issues that dated back to the European agenda or in which the focus was mainly organizational, and not exactly a political priority.

Within the scope of the presidency's responsibilities, the focus of the Portuguese presidency fell on organization, administration, coordination and also, partially, agenda-setting. The exercise of its representational role was not relevant. As to its mediation/negotiation functions, it performed its duties according to traditional norms and patterns, unable even to achieve success in the Delors II Package negotiations (one of its priorities). The defence of national interests, obviously present, was limited to its priorities, albeit with little ambition, since the main goal was to secure external credibility within Europe. In terms of leadership, with the exception of the reforms to the Common Agricultural Policy (CAP Portugal), there was no significant activity in any other dossier.

On the whole, with its first presidency in 1992, Portugal basically sought to demonstrate its capacity to carry out the activities of a European presidency in terms of organization, administration or coordination, or, in other words, that it measured up to its status as a full member of the EEC. This goal was entirely achieved, since the image that Portugal projected, as a small country, newly arrived in the EEC and exercising its first presidency, was one of competence, effectiveness and impartiality; therefore, that of a country that had fully earned its European credentials.

In that sense, if we use Elgström's classification,[51] Portugal followed an 'accommodating' strategy. The sociological approach would say that it adapted itself to the norm, since doing so was part of the appropriate conduct that Portugal considered other States were expecting of the Portuguese presidency. The presidency pursued, more than anything else, its external reputation, and in that sense it sought to accommodate its interests to European interests and fully comply with the norms of impartiality and efficiency. And this was rendered relatively easy, firstly because there were no strong national interests, and secondly because the emphasis of the presidency was essentially administrative and not motivated by initiative, political leadership or agenda-

---

[50] Ministério dos Negócios Estrangeiros, *Portugal 92*, pp. 27–29.
[51] Ole Elgström, p. 12.

setting concerns. In Kirchner's classification,[52] the Portuguese presidency followed a style of compromise and brokerage, and not an agenda-setting role. Thus, Portugal adopted a competitive and 'accommodating' strategy and sought mainly relative advantages, since the subjects of its interest did not warrant any specific focus or it did not have capacity to impose them and thus gain absolute advantages.

The rationalist approach, on the contrary, would say that Portugal assumed that attitude because it was a condition for the external credibility and prestige of the country and, therefore, corresponded precisely to the fundamental goal of national interests. The presidency was a unique opportunity for Portugal to defend its interests,[53] and not only to demonstrate its efficiency in the organization of the presidency, but also to favour a number of dossiers that were important for domestic reasons, such as the Delors II Package or the CAP.

The second Portuguese presidency (2000)

The second Portuguese presidency of the EU, in 2000, was carried out in a completely different context.[54] Portugal had completed almost a decade of European convergence, with economic and social modernization and a speedy Europeanization of its policies, and the country was going through an unprecedented period of Euro-enthusiasm.[55] Contrary to what happened in the first presidency, Portugal was able to convey the image of a country comfortably settled within the EU, a country endowed with a Portuguese idea for Europe and able to mobilize its peers to build the future of the European project. In 2000, Europe had been defined as the top priority in the scale of national interests, and it is in that context that the second Portuguese presidency was initiated.[56]

At the economic and social level, the major goal, achieved in the March 2000 European Council, was the approval of the Lisbon Strategy, a declaration of principles that sought to make the European Union the world's leading economy within a decade. Through the promotion of social, educational and environmental policies, the Lisbon Strategy sought to make the European economic area more competitive and better prepared for the challenges of globalization. Although their goals were important for the affirmation of Europe in the twenty-first century, the proposals approved in Lisbon were never put into practice, largely because the method of application skirted the traditional formulae of community integration, that is, its binding obligations.

[52] Emil Joseph Kirchner, pp. 105–09.
[53] Ole Elgström and Jonas Tallberg, p. 192.
[54] The Government was headed by António Guterres, with Jaime Gama as Foreign Minister and Francisco Seixas da Costa as Secretary of State for European Affairs.
[55] Nuno Severiano Teixeira, p. 20.
[56] Jaime Gama, *Política externa portuguesa (1999-2002)* (Lisbon: MNE, 2002), p. 291. See also João Pedro da Silveira Carvalho, 'Prioridades e resultados da Presidência do Conselho da UE', *Europa Novas Fronteiras*, 7 (2000), 14–23.

In the institutional sphere, in the course of the Intergovernmental Conference (IGC), the Portuguese presidency launched the idea of the Open Method of Coordination, thus contributing to the institutional improvement of the EU. Institutionally, the main issue was the reform of the institutions, and the main European goal was the improvement of the EU's institutional system, so as to adapt Brussels to the Eastern enlargement. In that context, the Intergovernmental Conference in Nice,[57] in 2000, despite its purpose having been only that of solving the issues remaining from the Amsterdam Treaty, marked the beginning of the pressure, from the bigger countries, to have their relative power acknowledged and reflected in vote weighting in the European decision-making process. To culminate this period of European enthusiasm in Portugal, the Nice IGC allowed the Portuguese presidency to assume a leadership role in relation to the small- and medium-sized European states, in order to defend their interests in the face of the bigger powers' demand for a reinforcement of their size in vote weighting. This role was important in the negotiations for institutional reform and undoubtedly represented one of the most active moments of Portugal's participation in the process of European integration.[58]

As regards foreign policy, the Portuguese presidency sought to develop 'the reinforcement of the Union's capacity for external affirmation',[59] by taking advantage of Portugal's historic relations with the regions traditionally connected to its national interests, in favour of the international presence of the European Union. Apart from the approval of the Common Strategy for the Mediterranean and the launch of the EU–India Strategy, the two top priorities of the Portuguese presidency — both of which met with success — revolved around Africa: the EU–ACP Cotonou Agreement and the organization of the first Africa–EU Summit.[60] An increasing shift of focus towards EU political, institutional and foreign policy matters is thus noticeable, at least to the degree enjoyed by the economic and social issues, that had been top priorities in the first presidency.

Economic issues continued to figure as Portuguese priorities but, from this point onwards, institutional, political and foreign policy matters also acquired increasing relevance. This was definitely an indication of a change in the Portuguese position which meant that the European project would thenceforth also address eminently political concerns.[61]

[57] On the Portuguese position see Francisco Seixas da Costa, 'Portugal e o Tratado de Nice: notas sobre a estratégia negocial', *Negócios Estrangeiros*, 1 (2001), 40–70.
[58] António Goucha Soares, 'Portugal e a adesão às Comunidades Europeias: 20 anos de integração europeia', in *España e Portugal: veinte años de integración europea*, ed. by Rafael García Pérez and Luís Lobo-Fernandes (Salamanca: Tórculo Edicións, 2007), pp. 69–83 (p. 77).
[59] Jaime Gama, *Política externa portuguesa (1999–2002)* (Lisbon: MNE, 2002), p. 72.
[60] Ministério dos Negócios Estrangeiros, *Portugal na União Europeia. Décimo Sexto Ano (2001)* (Lisbon: MNE, 2003), p. 11.
[61] Laura C. Ferreira-Pereira, 'Portugal e a Presidência da União Europeia (1992–2007)', *Relações Internacionais*, 20 (2008), 131–43.

Organization and coordination duties had an even greater weight than in the first presidency, due to the larger number of state members involved, the greater role of the European Parliament, the temporary frailty of the Commission, the larger number of Council formations at the various levels, and the wider reach of the Union's areas of competence. These duties were performed as competently and effectively as in the first presidency, although that was no longer a set goal, but something justly taken for granted, which did not require demonstration. Portugal had already won external credibility and its European credentials. Negotiation functions were carried out to a high degree, given the number of dossiers for the weighty array of Summits, particularly the more politically sensitive ones, such as the Africa–EU Summit, due to the specific group of states involved and the variety of clashing viewpoints. As to the initiative and leadership functions, the Portuguese presidency had a high profile and a degree of influence that exceeded the country's geographical size and weight in the context of the Union. It performed its role in the *open method of coordination* dossier, in the Lisbon Strategy, at the Africa–EU Summit, and particularly, in its leadership of minor countries during the Treaty of Nice debate on institutional reform.

In this second presidency, Portugal assumed a less administrative and more political profile, presenting a Portuguese idea for Europe and seeking to leave its mark on the European integration process. The emphasis and the goals were less administrative in nature and related more to negotiation, initiative and leadership. And Portugal sought, for the first time, to project its interests in the European process. Hence, the rationalist approach is useful to explain the behaviour of the Portuguese presidency at two levels: the definition of priorities, largely conditioned by domestic policy, and the attempt to bring matters of national interest to the European agenda.

Presidencies usually use the powers conferred upon them — access to a range of instruments and information, which assures them an asymmetrical advantage over other actors — to influence the agenda and pursue their own interests. This is how the Portuguese position on economic and social issues can be explained, with the Lisbon Strategy, the institutional issues, the leadership of small countries in institutional reform, and external action, with the holding of the EU–Africa Summit, a geographical area of strategic interest to Portugal.[62]

The 2000 presidency also made use of a competitive strategy, albeit from a different position to that in 1992, seeking to obtain relative advantages, regardless of any absolute advantage it might have additionally obtained. On the other hand, it endeavoured to influence the agenda and project its interests, yet without ever breaking the norms of impartiality, which would have harmed its reputation.

The sociological approach, however, is no less useful in its invocation of the country's cultural and historical issues to explain the behaviour of the

---

[62] Geoffrey Edwards and Georg Wiessala, 'Conscientious Resolve: The Portuguese Presidency of 2000', *Journal of Common Market Studies*, 39 (2001), 43–49.

presidencies. In this sense, Portugal placed on the European agenda the issues of economic and social cohesion and employment, the institutional issues of small countries, and the Europe–Africa rapprochement, because these concerns echoed the deep roots and identity of the country.

This kind of agenda, however, is only possible when the country is already integrated and socialized in the European political system, has diplomatic capacities, has had positive past experiences and, through the use of informal relations or historical links, manages the conciliation of its individual interests and European interests — in a word, when it manages to make its national interests a part of European interests. That was not possible at the early stage of the first presidency in 1992, but was attained in the second presidency in 2000.

The exercise of the presidency was based on a logic of appropriateness,[63] and it is in the light of that logic, to a large extent, that we are able to understand the priorities of the Portuguese presidency in 2000, and the way Portugal conducted them. Once again, taking into account Kirchner's classification,[64] it appears that in carrying out its second presidency, Portugal assumed a compromising role in relation to enlargement; one of broker at the IGC that led to the Treaty of Nice; and of agenda-setter in the organization of the EU-Africa Summit.

The third Portuguese presidency (2007)

The conclusions of the Treaty of Nice and the EU's eastward enlargement have since 2001 marked a change in Portugal's attitude towards Europe and European integration. On the one hand, they signal the dawn of a decade of divergence from its European partners, and on the other, the beginning of the end of Euro-enthusiasm and the return to pragmatism.[65] However, despite these difficulties, during the first decade of the twenty-first century, Portugal did not return to the hard-boiled scepticism that characterized the first years of its European integration. Furthermore, the Portuguese attitude was guided by a responsible realism. The third Portuguese presidency of the European Union in 2007 evinced the political maturity of Portugal's participation in the European project, both at the EU's internal level and internationally.

At the domestic level and in the field of economy, the year 2007 concluded the first three-year cycle of governance, and the second semester was mainly marked by the preparation of the 2008–10 cycle of the Lisbon Strategy. Actually, this issue was one of the priorities of the Portuguese presidency, which worked throughout the whole semester in close articulation with the Commission and also with Slovenia, which would be responsible for conducting the proceedings for the preparation of the European Council in the spring of 2008.[66]

---

[63] James G. March and Johan P. Olsen, pp. 951–52.
[64] Emil Joseph Kirchner, pp. 105–09.
[65] Nuno Severiano Teixeira, p. 23.
[66] Ministério dos Negócios Estrangeiros, *Portugal na União Europeia, Vigésimo Segundo Ano (2007)* (Lisbon: MNE, 2009), p. 69.

But the top priority of the presidency,[67] in the institutional domain, was the conclusion of the political process of reforming the European Union, an effort which led to the signature of the Treaty of Lisbon on 13 December 2007. Inherited from the German presidency, the approval of the Treaty of Lisbon also became a priority of the Portuguese presidency, which played a relevant role in the final phase of the negotiating process.[68]

At an international level, the Portuguese presidency's priorities centred on the reinforcement and diversification of the EU's external action, with the organization of a series of summits. The EU–Brazil and the EU–Africa Summits stood out as top priorities and, of lesser relevance, the summits with Ukraine, Russia, ASEAN, China and India and the Euromed (Euro-Mediterranean) ministerial meetings.[69] Holding these summits contributed to strengthening the European Union's international presence, but also favoured Portugal's interests through the expansion of the EU's Strategic Partnerships to traditional areas of Portuguese strategic interest, namely the relations with Africa and Brazil.[70] Finally, there was the enlargement of the Schengen area, an issue of freedom, security and justice but with implications for the EU's external action.[71]

In its third presidency of the European Union, Portugal continued to undertake its functions of organizing and coordinating the presidency's work competently, leaving an impression, already consolidated in previous presidencies, of effectiveness and impartiality.

Negotiation functions were carried out at high level, which was demonstrated by the organization of eight summits during its six-month presidency. Among these, the Portuguese priority was, undoubtedly, the EU–Africa Summit in which Portugal represented an added value, not only to its foreign policy but also to the Union's external action. In this context, it proved not only its organizational but also its negotiation skills, and, at the same time, its capacity to project its national interests.

With respect to its initiative and leadership function, the role of the Portuguese presidency was relatively high-profile, especially if we consider the size and the weight of the country in the Union's context. The approval of the Treaty of Lisbon was the top priority and, to some extent, the political flag of the Portuguese presidency. It is true that the project was a legacy from the German presidency, but at the decisive stage of the negotiating process and in the conclusion of the agreement, the Portuguese presidency played

---

[67] The Government was headed by José Sócrates, with Luís Amado as Foreign Minister and Manuel Lobo Antunes as Secretary of State for European Affairs.
[68] Manuel Lobo Antunes, 'Presidência em balanço', *Relações Internacionais*, 17 (2008), 5–10.
[69] Ministério dos Negócios Estrangeiros, *Portugal na União Europeia, Vigésimo Segundo Ano*, pp. 18–19.
[70] Laura C. Ferreira-Pereira, pp. 131–43.
[71] Ministério dos Negócios Estrangeiros, *Portugal na União Europeia, Vigésimo Segundo Ano*, pp. 17–18.

a significant role and proved not only its negotiation but also its leadership skills. Throughout the Portuguese presidency, the President of the European Commission, José Manuel Durão Barroso, always supported the process.

Besides the performance of these duties, Portugal demonstrated a capacity to project the national interests in the European agenda with greater assertiveness than in the previous presidencies. It managed to do this, however, in strict compliance with the norms of neutrality/impartiality, converging national and European interests.[72]

To summarize, in its third presidency Portugal reiterated its administrative skills of organization and coordination but assumed an essentially political profile, performed negotiation and leadership duties, and revealed its capacity to bring national interests into the European agenda. In a word, it was a fully integrated country, with an idea of Europe capable of leaving its imprint on the process of European integration. In this sense, the realist approach would explain the behaviour of the Portuguese presidency by the placing, on the European agenda, of issues of relevance for the national interest, as was made clear in the EU–Africa Summit initiative, which was a priority goal and a 'major initiative' of the third Portuguese presidency.[73] However, the issue that came to be the presidency's top priority, the approval of the Treaty of Lisbon, needs to be accounted for by means of a different logic, since both national and European interests converged there.

During its third presidency, Portugal adopted three different strategies, in Elgström's typology.[74] In the first place, there were 'forcing' and problem-solving strategies, widely used in the negotiations that led to the Treaty of Lisbon and, to a certain extent, in the organization of the EU–Africa Summit. Key interests were at stake there, and the presidency made use of all means within its reach to further them. However, since concerns with reputation remained, the presidency was forced to forego a number of substantial concerns — such as the loss of weight for small member states in the new institutional architecture — and used the problem-solving strategy more often. Secondly, there was the competition strategy. The presidency had to take into account the norms of neutrality and, as such, favour the achievement of relative advantages, rather than absolute ones, and follow a competition strategy. Finally, it also followed an 'accommodating' strategy, insofar as it had to consider its European credentials in its negotiation and leadership functions.

On the other hand, the sociological approach would explain the success of the presidency with the argument that Portugal was fully integrated in the Union, familiar with the integration processes and performing its role in respect of the neutrality norm, due to its endorsement of European values and interests. The

---

[72] Ministério dos Negócios Estrangeiros, *Portugal na União Europeia, Vigésimo Ano (2005)* (Lisbon: MNE, 2008), p. 544.
[73] José Sócrates, 'Uma União mais forte para um mundo melhor', *Europa Novas Fronteiras*, 21 (2007), 9–18.
[74] Ole Elgström, pp. 1–17.

priority given to the EU–Africa and the EU–Brazil Summits is easily explained by Portugal's historic and national identity issues.

According to Kirchner's typology,[75] it could be argued that Portugal, in its third presidency, assumed all three different styles: compromise, mediation, and agenda-setting. Compromise and mediation, essentially, in the renegotiation of the Lisbon Strategy and the negotiations during the IGC that led to the Treaty of Lisbon, and agenda-setting in the summits with Africa and Brazil.

Conclusion

From the empirical study and the theoretical analysis of the three Portuguese presidencies, three fundamental tendencies stand out. Firstly, the politicization of priorities. Concerns in 1992 had to do mainly with economic and social cohesion: the Delors II Package and CAP. In 2000, there seems to have been a balance between economic and political priorities: the Lisbon Strategy and the institutional reform in the Treaty of Nice. And in 2007, priorities were essentially political and related to external action: the approval of the Treaty of Lisbon and the summits with Brazil and Africa that paved the way to joint strategies. Thus, priorities evolved from economic and social concerns to institutional and political options.

Secondly, the externalization of priorities. In 1992, priorities were conditioned by and directed towards domestic policy. The perspective was that of a newcomer to European integration and the question was how Portugal could benefit from Europe. In 2000, priorities evolved from the national sphere to the European sphere. The perspective was that of a fully integrated country endowed with a Portuguese vision for European integration. In 2007, priorities confirmed and reinforced that tendency and also took on the EU's external action dimension. These were the priorities of a country that knew how to bring its interests onto the European agenda and to integrate national and European interests. The general tendency is thus from the national sphere to the European sphere and from the European sphere to that of Europe within the world.

Finally, let us consider the presidency's profile. In 1992, the emphasis was placed on the administrative, organizational and coordination functions. In 2000, the profile was less administrative and more political, and the focus was centred on negotiation and leadership functions. In 2007, the profile was markedly political and, to the negotiation and leadership functions, that of agenda-setting was added. According to Kirchner's typology,[76] we may conclude, summarily, that the profile of the Portuguese presidency evolved from a compromising style, in 1992, to one of mediation, in 2000, and agenda-setting, in 2007.

---

[75] Emil Joseph Kirchner, pp. 105–09.
[76] Emil Joseph Kirchner, pp. 105–09.

The Legacies of Revolution: Path-Dependence and Economic Performance in Portugal

SEBASTIÁN ROYO

Suffolk University, Boston, MA

Introduction

In comparative context, Portugal has enjoyed its relative successes along with some disappointments. Indeed, the Portuguese economy had a strong performance during the initial years of European Union (EU) membership. However, this initial success ended with the adoption of the single currency, and since then Portugal has embarked on a clear process of economic divergence within the Euro area. Unlike the other European cohesion countries — Spain, Greece and Ireland — which experienced strong periods of economic growth and were able to bridge the gap with the EU average over the decade prior to the global financial crisis of 2008, Portugal was referred by the European Commission as the disappointing exception among the so-called catching-up countries.[1] This essay seeks to explain this divergence. It argues that Portugal's historic path-dependency, marked by the country's distinctive democratization and its semi-peripheral economy, is still shaping the country's democracy and economic performance. The decades that followed the democratic transition have not yet fully addressed the historical challenges posed by weaknesses in the economy, state and civil society; and distorted governance still persists with detrimental effects on economic performance, effects that came to the fore during the recent global financial crisis and led to the country's bailout.[2]

The main argument of this essay is that the distinctiveness of the Portugal's pathway from dictatorship to democracy, coupled with other crucial features of its recent political past, helped to set the stage for the subsequent economic

---

[1] See 'EMU@10: Successes and Challenges after 10 years of Economic and Monetary Union,' *Mimeo*, Brussels, 7 May 2008.

[2] The purpose of this article is not to address all the variables that have impacted Portugal's economic performance since the democratic transition. There are indeed many other economic, cultural, political and social variables (including immigration) that are not included in this analysis but have been the subject of other studies. Rather, following the focus of the special volume on the legacies of the Revolution, this article seeks to assess how Portugal's revolutionary transition set the stage for the subsequent economic challenges that the country experienced. Hence, it focuses on a narrower set of factors associated with the legacies of the Revolution.

challenges that the country experienced following accession to European Monetary Union in 1999. Democracy was established but it was rooted in a distinctive socio-political experience that marked the resulting political and economic systems. Indeed, the radical socialist project, which predominated at the time of the Revolution, had a transformative impact in the country, and it led to a very socially and economically progressive Constitution that framed the choices of the political and economic actors for years to come, and hence impacted economic policy-making in subsequent decades. However, some of its more radical elements ultimately hindered the country's economic performance.[3]

The first part of this article examines Portugal's economic performance at the dawn of the new millennium. The second part analyses the impact of the revolutionary democratic transition on several dimensions that affected economic performance, namely justice, fiscal policy, political stability, governance structures, educational attainment, and labour performance and competitiveness.[4]

Portugal at the Dawn of the Twenty-first Century

Portugal's economic performance in the 1990s was remarkable. Between 1994 and 2000, real GDP growth (export-led but also boosted by private consumption and fixed investment) averaged more than 3% annually and economic expansion continued for seven years. In 1996, the fifth year of expansion, GDP growth reached almost 4%, and in 2000 it was still 3.25% (see Table 1). The unemployment rate also fell, reaching a record low of around 4% in 2000 (one of the lowest in Europe), and inflation was brought down to just over 2% in 1999. Portugal was also able to meet the Maastricht criteria for fiscal deficit following the consolidation efforts prior to 1997, which brought the deficit down to 2.5% of GDP. Some of the important factors that contributed to this performance were the transformation of the financial sector — largely spurred by EU directives on interest rate deregulation — liberalization of the regulatory framework, privatization, the EU funding of projects, and the freeing of international capital

---

[3] The 1976 constitution was a charged ideological document with references to socialism and a socialist economy, which restricted business activity and private investment. For instance, it proclaimed that the object of the republic was 'to ensure the transition to socialism', and urged the state to 'socialize the means of production and abolish the exploitation of man by man', and to 'direct its work toward the socialization of medicine and the medico-pharmaceutical sectors.'

[4] This article borrows from and builds upon: Sebastián Royo, 'Spain and Portugal in the EU: The Limits of Convergence', in *The European Union and the Member States*, ed. by Eleanor E. Zeff and Ellen B. Pirro (NY: Lynne Rienner, 2015), pp. 189–208; Sebastián Royo, 'The Limits of Convergence: Portugal in the European Union', *South European Society & Politics*, 18.2 (2013), 197–216 ; *Portugal in the Twenty-first Century: Politics, Society and Economics*, ed. by Sebastián Royo (Lanham, MD: Lexington Books, 2011); Sebastián Royo, 'Portugal's Experience in the European Union: Lessons for the Newcomers', in *Portugal in the European Union*, ed. by Laura Ferreira-Pereira (New York: Routledge, 2014), pp. 193–208.

movements. The privatization programme, one of the most ambitious in Europe at the time (more than one hundred firms were sold), was also a contributing factor because it brought in much needed capital and investment. In the run-up to the launch of the euro in 1999, the advantages of European Monetary Union (EMU) membership were clear as Portugal benefited from low interest rates and low inflation, which encouraged economic growth. Portuguese businesses benefited as well from the increase in cross-border trade, lower transaction costs, and from the stability of using a global currency, increased competition, and enhanced productivity gains; they generated revenues that averaged more than 2% of GDP per year.

The performance of the labour market was also very satisfactory. Real wage flexibility facilitated labour market adjustments, and access to atypical forms of employment, such as self-employment, made it possible to circumvent rigid regulations. In addition, regulatory reforms and new policy initiatives contributed to improving education and training, modifying the legal regime governing redundancies, reducing the compensation that companies had to pay to dismiss workers, changing the unemployment benefit system to avoid the unemployment 'trap', and bringing social security contributions for self-employed into line with those for employees. A high degree of wage flexibility, active employment policies, and the increasing use of more flexible forms of employment, such as fixed-term contracts, were all credited for the low unemployment (4.0% in 2000, down from 7.3% in 1996) and relatively high employment rates (the participation rate was 71.3% by 2000). Moreover, the social concertation policies of the 1990s contributed to social peace and wage moderation. For instance, in the Social Pact of 1996, management and labour reached binding commitments that facilitated reforms and wage restraint.[5]

However, from 1998 onwards, this performance started to deteriorate (see Table 1). As in other Eurozone countries, EMU membership may have offered too much protection by shielding the country against attacks (financial markets failed to distinguish among Eurozone countries), thereby allowing successive Portuguese governments to avoid the necessary reforms that would have fostered the country's productivity and competitiveness, and making it possible for them to postpone the necessary measures to reduce fiscal imbalances. This led to poor economic performance, particularly during the years prior to the global financial crisis of 2008.

The economic boom pushed wages up, and from 1999 there was increasing wage drift, which hindered competitiveness. The period of disinflation was halted as a result of increasing demand and the Expo 98, and inflation increased 2.8% by the end of 1998; the trade deficit also deteriorated, from 5.4% of GDP in 1997 to 6.6% in 1999. The harmonized Consumer Prices Index (CPI) reached

---

[5] 'Social concertation' refers to cooperation between trade unions, governments and employers in public policy-making. See Sebastián Royo, *A New Century of Corporatism?* (Westport, CT: Praeger, 2002).

over 4% in early 2001 (above the EU average), pushed by higher oil prices and a weaker euro. Furthermore, economic growth also started to slow, dragged down by the ending of major infrastructure projects and Expo 98. The onset of EMU membership led to a progressive easing of monetary conditions and a sharp decline in interest rates. This happened, however, at a time of high consumer demand, in which domestic credit was also booming and the current account deficit was widening (it remained at around 10% of GDP up to 2002). Access to EMU in 1999 did not alleviate the situation because Portugal was in a more advanced position in the cycle than the other EMU member states (the country was experiencing a credit boom and signs of overheating were starting to emerge), and now monetary policy was in the hands of the European Central Bank, which was making decisions based on developments in the entire EMU area. Indeed, there was a tightening of monetary conditions after the ECB started to gradually raise rates, from November 1999 on.

Furthermore, the end of the decade — which coincided with the country's accession to EMU (meaning that the pressure to fulfil the Maastricht criteria was no longer a powerful incentive) — also witnessed a slowdown in the fiscal consolidation efforts, which had led to the successful reduction of the fiscal deficit between 1994 and 1997 (there was an annual reduction of almost 1.2 percentage points, and the deficit was reduced to 2.5% by 1997). Yet, about half of this fiscal adjustment was the result of the reduction of the public debt burden facilitated by the lower interest rates and non-recurring receipts (such as the sale of mobile phone concessions in 2000). In fact, the primary surplus increased half a point per year between 1994 and 1997. There was no increase in taxes, and current expenditure on education, health, and social protection increased steadily.[6]

Reasons for the Portuguese Divergence

Historical legacies and the impact of the transition to democracy

A central argument of this article is that Portugal's economic performance in the years prior to the global financial crisis was impacted by the mode of the democratic transition and its distinctively progressive Constitution. The 'revolutionary period' of 1974–75 was the most complex phase of the transition, during which it was still unclear what kind of regime was to be established. During these two years, powerful tensions emerged within Portuguese society, but they began to subside in 1976, when a new constitution was approved and the first legislative and presidential elections were held. As noted by Lobo, Pinto and Magalhães, 'the nature of the transition left several legacies to the

---

[6] Data in this section is from the OECD, *OECD Economic Surveys: Portugal* (Paris: OECD, 1996, 1999, 2001 and 2006), and the IMF, *World Economic Outlook 2009* (Washington, DC: International Monetary Fund, 2009).

Table 1. Economic Performance Portugal 1997–2011: Source: IMF, World Economic Outlook, 2011

	Units	1998	1999	2000	2001	2002	2003	2004
Gross domestic product, constant prices	Percent change	4.852	3.841	3.925	2.016	0.759	-0.805	1.516
Output gap in percent of potential GDP	Percent of potential GDP	0.34	1.545	3.114	3.081	2.071	-0.242	-0.011
GDP based on purchasing-power-parity (PPP) share of world total	Percent	0.431	0.433	0.429	0.428	0.42	0.402	0.387
Inflation, average consumer prices	Percent change	2.213	2.167	2.807	4.41	3.677	3.257	2.508
Current account balance	Percent of GDP	-7.053	-8.464	-10.241	-9.9	-8.093	-6.103	-7.578
General government structural balance	Percent of potential GDP	-3.372	-2.792	-2.966	-4.321	-2.889	-2.953	-3.383
General government net lending/borrowing	Percent of GDP	-4.95	-4.4	-3.925	-4	-5	-6.25	-6.65
Unemployment rate	Percent of total labour force							

	Units	2005	2006	2007	2008	2009	2010	2011
Gross domestic product, constant prices	Percent change	0.91	1.368	1.872	0.043	-2.678	0.293	0.653
Output gap in percent of potential GDP	Percent of potential GDP	-0.208	0.181	1.171	0.404	-2.578	-2.39	-2.047
GDP based on purchasing-power-parity (PPP) share of world total	Percent	0.373	0.361	0.35	0.34	0.333	0.325	0.315
Inflation, average consumer prices	Percent change	2.129	3.043	2.425	2.651	-0.902	0.841	1.088
Current account balance	Percent of GDP	-9.481	-10.029	-9.429	-12.115	-10.057	-8.976	-10.165
General government structural balance	Percent of potential GDP	-5.995	-3.999	-3.193	-3.496	-7.813	-7.062	-6.515
General government net lending/borrowing	Percent of GDP	-6.051	-3.941	-2.652	-2.751	-9.334	-8.729	-7.537
Unemployment rate	Percent of total labour force	7.6	7.65	8	7.6	9.455	11.004	10.338

political system. First, the presence of the military, which had been determinant for the demise of the *Estado Novo*, demanded a stake in the new regime. [...] Second, the authoritarian right-wing nature of the *Estado Novo*, and especially the radicalization of the transition, guaranteed an ascendancy for the left-wing parties within the party system. Nonetheless, the conflicts between Socialist and Communist parties during the transition rendered any coalitions between the two major parties on the Left unviable'.[7] In particular, two specific characteristics of the democratic transition — the development of a progressive constitution, and the explosion of revolutionary mass mobilization in the country — distinguish the Portuguese case in ways that contributed to account for subsequent economic challenges.

The Constituent Assembly adopted the new constitution on 2 April 1976. This constitution had a strong socialist stance, and it was the outcome of a compromise between various factions that had been involved in the revolutionary period, led by the military and the parties that competed to determine the workings of the state and government, and it included workers' committees and residents' committees. It has since been amended seven times. One of the most significant amendments took place in 1982, with the votes of the right-wing government parties and the Socialist Party (PS), and it showed the shift in the balance of forces due to the decline in the power of the military, of revolutionary activists, and of the left in general. This reform circumscribed the powers of the President and subordinated the military to partisan political power. The Council of the Revolution was extinguished and its powers were re-distributed among other institutions which were set up (all dominated by the political parties), namely, a consultative body for the President (the Council of State) and a Constitutional Court to defend the Constitution.[8] The Constitutional reform of 1989, which resulted in the elimination of the constitutional obstacles to privatizations, crystallized Portuguese labour's defeat. This development took on its full significance when placed in the context of the programme of structural reforms, and the privatization process that intensified with subsequent governments.

In addition, the Constitution also had a critical political impact, with implications for policy-making and economic performance. It established a presidential system, and while Portuguese presidents do not have the powers of French presidents — or still less of US presidents — they have been able to block government proposals when they opposed them (particularly in the periods of 'cohabitation', when the country elected a president from a different party to the one in government). Indeed, one of the major features of the Portuguese presidential system has been the president's power to refer controversial

---

[7] Marina Costa Lobo, António Costa Pinto and Pedro Magalhães, 'The Political Institutions of Portuguese Democracy', in *Portugal in the Twenty-first Century: Politics, Society and Economics*, ed. by Sebastián Royo (Lanham, MD: Lexington Books, 2011), pp. 23–48 (pp. 25–26).
[8] Lobo, Pinto and Magalhães, pp. 30–31.

legislation to the Constitutional Court. For instance, in the second half of the 1980s, Mário Soares, who was elected President with the support of the PS and PCP, was able to restrain the reforming impetus of the PSD government then in power and safeguard the rights of workers. In 1986 he prevented the implementation of the labour reform approved by the PSD government by sending it to the Constitutional Court, which, as noted below, declared it out of conformity with the regime's constitution. He used this power forty-three times from 1986, and succeeded two-thirds of the time in forcing the PSD to redraft important legislation.[9] The power to refer parliament- and cabinet-initiated bills or cabinet-issued decrees for prior judicial review by the Constitutional Tribunal has been an important power exercise by the presidents, as noted in Table 2.

	Parliament-Initiated Laws	Cabinet-Initiated Laws	Total per Mandate	Total per President
Soares I	11 (8)	5 (5)	16 (13)	43 (30)
Soares II	17 (14)	10 (3)	27 (17)	
Sampaio I	3 (2)	2 (1)	5 (3)	16 (11)
Sampaio II	8 (8)	3 (0)	11 (8)	
Total	39 (32)	20 (9)	59 (41)	59 (41)

TABLE 2. Constitutional referral of laws per president; laws that were considered unconstitutional in parentheses. Source: Octavio Amorim Neto and Marina Costa Lobo, 'Portugal's Semi-Presidentialism (Re)Considered', in *Portugal in the Twenty-first Century: Politics, Society and Economics*, ed. by Sebastián Royo (Lanham, MD: Lexington Books, 2011), 49–68 (p. 62).

Another presidential power, which was enhanced by the 1982 constitutional reform, is the veto power, which has served as an *ex post* mechanism to control the cabinet and parliament, but has also hindered policy-making. Table 3 displays the number of vetoes issued per president and legislature, along with the total number of laws passed. As we shall see, both presidential constitutional powers had implications for economic policy-making.

In addition, the inherited Portuguese administrative tradition, characterized by a considerable weight of the state in society and a tradition of centralization in the state administration, was substantially reinforced by the constitution. Indeed, Portugal remains one of the most centralized countries in Western Europe, given that there is no intermediate locus of power between local and national government, with local government having very little power or resources. The decades following the Carnation Revolution witnessed the

---

[9] Daniel Nataf, *Democratization and Social Settlements: The Politics of Change in Contemporary Portugal* (New York: SUNY Press, 1995), p. 191.

President	Legislature	Largest cabinet parties	No. laws proposed	Political vetoes and constitutionality-related vetoes	% vetoes per mandate	% vetoes by president
Eanes	1976–1980	PS*	341	10	2.9	2.1
	1980–1983	PSD-CDS	119	5	4.2	
	1983–1985	PS-PSD	303	1	0.3	
Soares	1985–1987	PSD	163	3	1.8	2.9
	1987–1991	PSD	405	10	2.5	
	1991–1995	PSD	305	12	3.9	
Sampaio	1995–1999	PS	479	5	1.0	2.3
	1999–2002	PS	198	6	3.0	
	2002–2005	PSD-CDS	250	10	4.0	

TABLE 3. Presidential vetoes per president and legislature
Source: Amorin Neto and Costa Lobo, p. 62.
Notes: *Together with the CDS in the 2nd cabinet.

growth of the state both in the economy as well as in its welfare capacity. Not only that, the role of the state in expenditure terms has increased substantially, almost doubling as a proportion of GDP in the last twenty years. Part of this increase is explained by the large increase in the role of the state as a provider of social services, including education, health, and social security.[10]

Impact on justice

The specific characteristics of the democratic transition have also impacted fundamental areas of state action such as justice, which is crucial for the effective working of the economy. Indeed, there is a wide consensus that Portugal faces a crisis in the area of justice, and there is enormous popular frustration at the performance of the judicial system: the courts are overburdened with legal proceedings, and court decisions very often extend beyond what would be a reasonably acceptable timeline for the achievement of justice. At the same time, there is a widespread feeling throughout the country that there is a dual system of justice: one for powerful people, who tend to receive lenient treatment in criminal proceedings, and a different one for poor people.[11]

The constitutional reform in 1997 sought to address the perception of the Constitutional Court's lack of independence vis-à-vis parliament in general, and the political parties in particular, by extending the terms of the Constitutional Court's justices to nine years and making them non-renewable (they were

[10] Lobo, Pinto and Magalhães, pp. 39–40.
[11] António Goucha Soares, 'Portugal: An Incomplete Europeanization', in *Portugal in the Twenty-first Century: Politics, Society and Economics*, ed. by Sebastián Royo (Lanham, MD: Lexington Books, 2011), pp. 121–44 (p. 128).

previously six years long and renewable). However, this has not ended the recurrent criticisms made by the career judiciary about the 'politicization' of the Court. Another area of almost permanent contention has been the organization of the judicial system itself. During the Portuguese democratic transition important reforms were introduced in order to ensure the independence of courts and judges. In 1976, a Supreme Judicial Council was entrusted with all decisions pertaining to the promotions, transfers and evaluation of judges, including disciplinary actions against them. The 1982 and 1997 constitutional reforms changed the composition of this Council in order to combine judges (seven judges are elected by their respective peers) and appointees (two members appointed by the President of the Republic; seven members appointed by the Parliament, and one ex-officio member — the President of the Council holds this position by virtue of being President of the Supreme Court). This change resulted, however, in the insulation of judges from any kind of accountability for performance and the closure of the profession in relation to lateral entries from qualified lawyers outside the career.

In any case, a 'crisis of justice' continues as 'manifested in the rising number of pending processes, the decline in judicial productivity, the bias of the system's performance in favour of "repeat players", and the inability to effectively obtain convictions in many cases of corruption and "white-collar crime" uncovered by the press, which has led to a deadlock in the process of judicial reform that, from the point of view of citizens, has played no small role in breeding a growing mistrust vis-à-vis the judicial branch and the overall performance of courts.'[12] Hence, it is not surprising that cases of corruption, mismanagement of public goods, tax evasion, or illicit financing of political parties often end merely on the basis of legal technicalities, with no criminal sanction for those indicted after a long criminal investigation. In other words, it is 'a legal system that is unable to fulfil its mission'.[13]

Impact on domestic fiscal policies

Lax monetary policy also played a significant role in the slowdown of the convergence process prior to EMU accession.[14] Indeed, one of the fundamental reasons for the poor performance of the Portuguese economy between 1999 and 2006 was the lack of fiscal discipline and the failure of *ad hoc* measures to control the deficit. It is now widely accepted that increases in government consumption adversely affect long-term growth,[15] and also that while fiscal consolidation may have short-term costs in terms of activity, those costs can be minimized by implementing credible and consistent decisions.

---

[12] Lobo, Pinto and Magalhães, pp. 42–43.
[13] Goucha Soares, p. 131.
[14] Frank Barry, 'Economic Integration and Convergence Processes in the EU Cohesion Countries,' *Journal of Common Market Studies*, 41.5 (2003), 1–25.
[15] See Daniel J. Mitchell, 'The Impact of Government Spending on Economic Growth', *Executive Summary Backgrounder: Published by The Heritage Foundation*, No. 1831 (31 March 2005), pp. 1–18.

As we have seen, the Portuguese economy experienced a boom in the second half of the 1990s, when nominal short-term interest rates converged with those set by the ECB. In both cases, they fell more rapidly than did inflation, and the simultaneous processes of financial liberalization and increasing competition that took place at the same time — which contributed to increasing domestic demand, and housing demand in particular — further boosted their impact. The expansion in these years was driven largely by internal demand. This boom also coincided with a period of international expansion. The growth, however, would have required a concomitant prudent fiscal policy, which in the case of Portugal did not take place. On the contrary, the cyclically adjusted primary balance fell from 1.2% of GDP in 1994–96 to -0.6% in 1999–2001. At the same time, the combination of expansionary fiscal policies and insufficient structural reforms did not prepare the country for the economic downturn.

Indeed, there is widespread consensus that Portugal's biggest mistake was its 'chronic fiscal misbehaviour'.[16] Vítor Constâncio, then Governor of the Bank of Portugal, has acknowledged that 'in 2001, we had these big shocks to growth, tax revenues dropped and suddenly we were in a situation of an excessive deficit. [...] The sudden emergence of budget problems led to a big revision of expectations about the future.'[17] Largely as a result of this revision of expectations, the Portuguese economy contracted by 0.8% in 2003. The Portuguese experience shows that countries wishing to join the Eurozone need to have a 'comfortable budget position because that will give room for manoeuvre once inside.'[18] Not surprisingly, of the cohesion countries, the ones that did better in the last decade and a half have been those that have maintained fiscal discipline — Ireland and Spain — which have either maintained a budget surplus or reduced their budget deficits to comply with the Stability and Growth Pact-SGP, while reducing their total expenditures as a proportion of GDP. Portugal, as we have seen, was the exception.

The pro-cyclical policy stance did not bode well for the subsequent slowdown of the economy because Portugal was left with little fiscal leeway to apply counter-cyclical measures once the crisis hit. In order to improve its margin for manoeuvre, Portugal should have reduced the weight of the public sector and also implemented structural reforms to check the growth of current expenditures, which would have allowed for a reduction in tax pressure. The country would have needed to achieve a significant surplus to ensure balance for the budget over the cycle, but unfortunately this did not happen.

In the end, as another legacy of the revolutionary transition, Portugal lacked the appropriate fiscal constitution — the set of institutions that enforce the

---

[16] Martin Wolf, 'Struggling to Tackle Bad Fiscal Behaviour', *Financial Times*, 8 April 2008, special section on *Investing in Portugal*, pp. 1–2.
[17] Interview with Vítor Constâncio, Governor of the Bank of Portugal: 'Concerns about divergence "overlook ability to change"', *Financial Times*, 16 May 2008, p. 2.
[18] Interview with Vítor Constâncio, Governor of the Bank of Portugal: 'Tough cuts to strengthen confidence,' in *Financial Times*, 8 April 2008, special section on *Investing in Portugal*, p. 2.

social contract, which secures citizens' mutual protection and welfare — and this led to unsustainable fiscal policies. This was also compounded by the deficient administration that undermined the social legitimacy of taxes and prevented the reform of the public administration.[19]

Impact on Policy Stability

The Portuguese political system also failed to deliver policy stability and government continuity in the years prior to the crisis, with deleterious consequences for economic policy continuity and performance. Indeed, there were four Prime Ministers (PMs) between 1995 and 2005, and three of them resigned before their terms were over, though for different reasons. António Guterres was PM from 28 October 1995 to 6 April 2002. During his first term, Portugal enjoyed a solid economic expansion and very successfully staged the Expo 98. However, the beginning of the economic crisis and the Hintze Ribeiro disaster of March 2001, in which 70 people died when the bridge of that name collapsed, damaged his popularity and marred his second term. He resigned following the disastrous result for the Socialist Party in the December 2001 local elections, stating that 'I will resign to prevent the country from falling into a political swamp.'

Following a general election won by the opposition Social Democratic Party, the Social Democrat party leader José Manuel Durão Barroso became PM on 6 April 2002. He held the post until 17 July 2004, ruling in coalition with the Popular Party. He resigned when he was named President of the European Commission, at a time when the Portuguese economy was entering one of the worst phases of the economic crisis — a decision for which he was very severely criticized. Pedro Miguel Santana Lopes replaced him from his own party, and held the position from 29 June 2004 to 12 March 2005. His short tenure was marred by controversies over his unusual election (he was not elected by popular vote), the fact that he was not a member of parliament (he was Mayor of Lisbon when he was selected PM), and continuous PR fiascos, which led President Sampaio to dissolve Parliament and call for early elections. The Socialist José Sócrates won the general election in a landslide victory with an overwhelming absolute majority in parliament (45% of the vote and 121 seats), for the first time since the democratic transition, to become PM on 12 March 2005. He was re-elected in September 2009, but resigned on 21 June 2011 after his government's austerity measures were rejected by a vote in parliament, leading to the parliamentary election of 2011 won by the Social Democrats.[20] These constant changes up to 2005 made economic policy continuity more problematic and, more importantly, they made the implementation of reforms in the face of popular opposition very difficult.

[19] António Braga de Macedo, 'Portugal's European Integration: The Good Student with a Bad Fiscal Constitution', in *Spain and Portugal in the European Union: The First 15 Years*, ed. by Sebastián Royo and Paul C. Manuel (London: Frank Cass, 2003), pp. 169–94 (p. 184).
[20] The period of stability under PM Sócrates, which falls outside of the scope of this article, led to significant reforms. See Royo, 'Spain and Portugal in the EU: The Limits of Convergence'.

Furthermore, the position of finance minister became a revolving door, bringing instability to the economic policy portfolio, with ministers often resigning in protest at their inability to hold sway over their colleagues and control fiscal policies and expenditures. Between 1990 and 2005, there were ten ministers of finance (Table 4), and on average they each held the position for less than two years. The problem was compounded by the finance minister's limited powers over the budget. Indeed, according to a recent study of all the EU15 finance ministers, the Portuguese minister had the least amount of control over the formulation, approval, and implementation of the budget.[21]

21 July 2005	Fernando Teixeira dos Santos
12 March 2005	Luís Campos e Cunha
17 July 2004	António Bagão Félix
6 April 2002	Maria Manuela Ferreira Leite
3 July 2001	Guilherme d'Oliveira Martins
25 October 1999	Joaquim Augusto Nunes de Pina Moura
28 October 1995	António Luciano Pacheco de Sousa Franco
7 December 1993	Eduardo Almeida Catroga
31 October 1991	Jorge Braga de Macedo
4 January 1990	Luís Miguel Beleza

TABLE 4. Ministers of Finance, 1990–2008

This problem extends to other critical areas, such as education: Maria Isabel Girão de Melo Veiga Vilar Alçada, the Minister of Education in 2009, was the twenty-eighth education minister in thirty-three years.

In the end, the credibility of economic policies (and fiscal policies in particular) was undermined by the relative political instability that prevailed in Portugal in the first years of this century.

Impact on governance structures

Portugal was exposed late to Weberian principles of neutral civic administration and it has a long history of neopatrimonialism. The country's political development was hindered by clientelistic regimes throughout the nineteenth and the first part of the twentieth centuries. Despite radical social transformations the Revolution did not lead to a change in this situation, as clientelism and patronage have persisted. Political and institutional instability prevented the construction of a Weberian state until 1987, and it was only under the government of Cavaco Silva (1987–91) that the process of institutional reform intensified. Yet, this change was already behind the modern public management systems that were established in other European countries at that time. The

---

[21] Mark Halleberg, Rolf Strauch and Juergen von Hagen, 'The Design of Fiscal Rules and Forms of Governance in European Union Countries', in *ECB Working Paper*, 419 (December 2004).

consequence has been a persistence of civil administrative subcultures based on the Weberian neutral services, supporters of the new public management, and also clientelistic and neopatrimonial forms of behaviour. This has been very detrimental for the country. In the context of a weak state, an underperforming economy and a weak society, this system has hindered effective governance and policy-making and it has hurt the country's ability to build a sustainable social market economy. The state has been the focus of redistribution, but it still lacks the economic basis to sustain this system. At the same time, the country's labour markets lack a strong social security system. Indeed, labour market reforms have emphasized deregulation and flexibilization, and they have left aside the accompanying social welfare policies that characterize the Nordic flexicurity systems. Lastly, industrial relations are still underdeveloped with a large informal economy that remains largely unprotected, and a weak state capacity to enforce compliance with labour laws. In sum, the persisting distorted form of governance keeps undermining the country's political and economic foundations.[22]

Impact on educational attainment

Another area in which the specific characteristics of the democratic transition have also failed to deliver effective state action has been in the educational system, which is crucial for the effective working of an economy. EU funds have been used to co-finance projects improving infrastructure and human resources, and to help in areas such as technological innovation and investment. EU-funded investments in infrastructure have improved accessibility and from a supply-side effect have contributed to boost productivity. Yet the educational attainment performance of the country has been disappointing: a large proportion of young students leave school before completing secondary education, and the achievements of students in PISA (Programme for International Student Assessment) are among the poorest in the OECD.

According to the OECD, the performance of Portuguese secondary school students was among the weakest in the developed world, and the dropout rate one of the highest.[23] Between 1995 and 2005 half of Portugal's youth left school at 15, before completing secondary education, and the current dropout rate is still 40%, more than double the EU average (at 16%). Furthermore, reading and maths skills among 15-year-olds are among the weakest in Europe: Portuguese students number between 22% and 33% performing at or below the level of 'very basic', while only about 5% achieve the highest international standards. The problem also affected higher education: in 2008, the percentage of the population with a university education was only 12% (up from 2% in 1974 when democracy

---

[22] José Magone, *Politics in Contemporary Portugal: Democracy Evolving* (Boulder, CO: Lynne Rienner, 2014), pp. 40–41.
[23] OECD, 2006, p. 6.

was restored), compared with an EU average of 24%. In order to increase this figure, students must stay in school longer and complete secondary education. According to the IMF, Portugal's low educational standards, job skills, research and development investment, and computer use were among the greatest challenges for regaining lost competitiveness.[24] Indeed, the educational level of the workforce has to reflect the shift from low-cost, unskilled manufacturing to more value-added sectors.

While illiteracy, which affected a fifth of the 15- to 64-year-olds in 1974, has been virtually eradicated, the education system failed to limit the repetition of underperformance from one generation to another within families and to foster the necessary inter-generational mobility. This problem is compounded by the low educational standards of many parents, who left school at the age of fifteen and still make education a low priority for their families. Poor schooling results have a ripple effect on productivity, research and innovation, which helps account for Portugal's weak competitiveness and slow growth. It is therefore critical for Portugal to narrow this 'human capital gap' in order to improve productivity and resume 'catching up'. The problem, however, has been not so much insufficient funding, but the system's low efficiency. Public spending per student was close to the European average and the education budget doubled during the decade prior to the global financial crisis, but the number of students fell. Most Eastern European countries spent much less but still achieved similar or better results.[25] One of the main problems is that teachers' salaries accounted for 93% of spending (compared with 75% in the OECD). Therefore, it is not lack of resources, but how they are being used. Not surprisingly, the Portuguese PM, José Sócrates, recognized that 'problems like the budget deficit can be solved in two or three years, [but] our structural deficit in education and training is a much bigger challenge'.[26]

Impact on labour performance and competitiveness

An additional characteristic of the Portuguese democratic transition, with important implications for economic performance, was the explosion of revolutionary mass mobilization. In other countries, such as Spain or Greece, the relative moderation and gradualism of the democratization process favoured the creation of relationships of trust among emerging workers' organizations and employers. These actors submerged their objectives within the overall project of gradual democratization. In Portugal, however, the revolutionary phases of the democratization process fostered the radicalization

---

[24] From 'Lisbon leads the Union while lagging in performance leagues', *Financial Times*, 3 July 2007, p. 4.
[25] OECD, 2006, p. 6.
[26] From 'Lisbon leads the Union while lagging in performance leagues', *Financial Times*, 3 July 2007, p. 4.

of workers and intensified class antagonisms.[27] This development has left a legacy of distrust among the actors that has lasted until today and has deepened the politicization of industrial relations. Indeed, Portuguese labour was a major actor during the transition process and participated actively in the development of the 1976 Constitution, which resulted in its pro-worker stance.[28] The consequence of this development has been that successive democratic governments faced constraints when they tried to reform labour laws to make them more favourable to business. For instance, as noted above, in 1987 the Portuguese Constitutional Court declared unconstitutional a labour reform approved by the PSD government. Consequently, the business point of view has never had the hegemonic influence that it had in countries such as Spain. Businesses were aware that they had to negotiate with labour to reform labour laws or bargain over wages.

As noted before, the country was successful in controlling wages during the decade following accession to the EU. However, the economic boom of the 1990s pushed wages up, and from 1999 there was increasing wage drift, which hindered competitiveness. Indeed, while Germany (and other EMU countries) implemented supply-side reforms to bring labour costs down (through wage restraint, payroll tax cuts, and productivity increases, making it the most competitive economy, with labour costs 13% below the Eurozone average), Portugal continued with the tradition of indexing wage increases to domestic inflation rather than the European Central Bank target, and they became the most expensive ones: Portugal had labour costs 23.5% above the EU average (followed by Spain with 16%, Greece with 14% and Italy with 5%).[29]

In this regard, Portugal provides interesting insights into the pitfalls of integration into EMU. As noted by Vítor Constâncio, then Governor of the Bank of Portugal, one of the main lessons from Portugal's experience is that 'countries used previously to high inflation and high interest rates are likely to experience an explosion in consumer spending and borrowing' upon joining the monetary union.[30] This spurt would make a downturn inevitable, particularly in cases such as Portugal, which is vulnerable to higher oil prices and increasing competition from developing countries like India and China. In Portugal strong demand stemmed from a sharp fall in interest rates, and it was further fuelled by expansive fiscal policies. Demand, however, was not followed by a parallel increase in supply, as it was hindered by low productivity

---

[27] Alan Stoleroff, 'The Portuguese Labour Movement and Industrial Democracy: From Workplace Revolution to a Precarious Quest for Economic Justice,' *Transfer*, 22.1 (2016), 101–19; and José Barreto and Reinhard Naumann, 'Portugal: Industrial Relations under Democracy', in *Industrial Relations in the New Europe*, ed. by Anthony Ferner and Richard Hyman (Oxford: Blackwell, 1998), pp. 395–425.

[28] Rafael Durán Muñoz, *Contención y transgresión: las movilizaciones sociales y el estado en las transiciones española y portuguesa* (Madrid: Centro de Estudios Políticos y Constitucionales, 2000).

[29] Royo, 'Spain and Portugal in the EU: The Limits of Convergence'. See also Glatzer's contribution to this special volume.

[30] Interview with Vítor Constâncio, Governor of the Bank of Portugal: 'Concerns about divergence "overlook ability to change"', in *Financial Times*, 16 May 2008, p. 2.

growth, which led to a significant increase in imports and high external deficits and debts. External indebtedness in turn has led to lower government income domestically. In the end, lower interest rates and the loosening of credit led to a credit boom that increased housing demand and household indebtedness. This boom led to higher wage increases (caused by the tightening of the labour market) and losses in external competitiveness, together with a shift from the tradable to the non-tradable sector of the economy, which includes such elements as electricity, water supply, all public services, hotel accommodation, real estate, construction and local transportation.[31]

Another related problem for Portugal was the dramatic erosion of its comparative advantage (exports represented 25.7% of GDP in 2004 and imports 29.3%). The emergence of major new players in world trade, like India and China, as well as the eastern enlargements of the European Union, were particularly damaging to the Portuguese economy, because these countries have lower labour costs and they competed with Portugal's traditional exports (as an exporter of relatively unsophisticated labour-intensive products). This led to losses in export market shares (aggravated by the appreciation of the euro, and the increase of unit labour costs relative to those in its trading competitors). At the same time Portugal's attempt to specialize in medium- and higher-technology products was also hindered by the accession of the Eastern European countries into the EU, who were moving into those sectors and also specializing in those products. Finally, it is important to note that many Portuguese economic groups adopted defensive growth strategies based on investment in non-tradable sectors, rather than internationalize.[32]

In the end, the country's ability to keep the lid on unit labour costs, rooted in the labour institutions inherited from the revolutionary transition, was insufficient to generate enough growth in exports to compensate for decreasing domestic demand. While easy access to cheap credit had boosted domestic demand, it also caused a shift of resources from tradables to non-tradables (services). This shift was further hastened by high wage increases (including the public sector) caused by a tighter labour market in the second half of the 1990s, which further hampered external competitiveness and productivity. The result was an imbalanced economy sustained by strong domestic demand that translated into higher imports (and external deficit).

Until 2000, the impact of wage increases was offset by high productivity growth — it grew at a yearly average of 2.2% between 1996 and 2000 — thus limiting the growth of unit labour costs. After 2000, however, the international expansionary cycle started to reverse, particularly in the EU, which is the leading market for Portuguese exports, where growth slowed to 1.4% between

---

[31] Orlando Abreu, 'Portugal's Boom and Bust: Lessons for Euro Newcomers', in *ECFIN Country Focus*, 3.16 (22 December 2006), p. 5.
[32] *Multinationals, Clusters and Innovation: Does Public Policy Matter?*, ed. by Ana Teresa Tavares and Aurora Teixeira (New York: Palgrave, 2008).

2001 and 2003 (compared to 2.8% between 1995 and 2000). This deceleration of the international economic cycle hit Portugal severely, and affected expectations among consumers and businesses.

Furthermore, some Portuguese sectors of the economy did not prepare well for the WTO liberalization of sectors, with major economic impact in the country, particularly footwear and textiles. The situation was compounded by the Asian crisis of the late 1990s, which affected mainly Thailand, Indonesia and South Korea, and led to the devaluation of those countries' currencies, further eroding the competitiveness of Portuguese exports. As a result, Portuguese exports of footwear and textiles fell from almost two thirds of total exports of goods between 1995 and 1996, to a little more than one third between 2004 and 2005, with the concurrent wave of dismissals and closures, which further dampened expectations and caused social problems, particularly in the north of the country, where these industries are based.[33]

Yet, while this article has emphasized the relative underperformance of Portugal's economy in terms of real convergence, it is important to highlight that Portugal has had a much stronger employment record, which has been the object of important work by scholars such as Robert M. Fishman, Oliver Blanchard, Juan F. Jimeno, Pedro Portugal, José da Silva Lopes, Gosta Esping-Andersen, David Cameron, and others. According to Fishman, there are three main reasons associated with the legacies of Portugal's democratic transition in the 1970s: the high level of the female participation rate; the availability of credit to small companies; and finally, the 'nature of the Portuguese welfare state which became increasingly "employment-friendly" in the 1990s.'[34]

Conclusion

This article has examined how Portugal's distinctive passageway from dictatorship to democracy, coupled with other crucial features of its recent political past, helped to set the stage for the subsequent economic challenges that the country experienced following accession to the European Monetary Union in 1999. It has argued that the absence of macroeconomic policy stability, lack of consensus among the leading political parties, poor performance in educational attainment, insufficient fiscal consolidation, and the erosion of comparative advantage help account for the poor economic performance that eventually led to the 2008 crisis and the country's bailout. These problems were largely the result of the country's distinctive revolutionary transition.

The effects of the recent global financial crisis on the country have been

---

[33] Abreu, 'Portugal's Boom and Bust', pp. 3–4; and Martin Wolf, 'Struggling to tackle bad fiscal behaviour', *Financial Times*, 8 April 2008, special section on *Investing in Portugal*, pp. 1–2.

[34] Robert Fishman, 'Legacies of Democratizing Reform and Revolution: Portugal and Spain Compared' (paper presented at the Annual Meeting of the American Political Science Association, Chicago, IL, September 2004), available online at <http://citation.allacademic.com/meta/p_mla_apa_research_citation/0/6/1/6/8/pages61689/p61689-1.php>.

devastating.[35] As noted in the Introduction, since coming to power in 2015, Prime Minister Costa's PS government has implemented policies that seek to generate growth, fiscal consolidation and social cohesion, and it has outperformed initial forecasts. In 2016 the economy grew by a slow but still positive 1.4%, the deficit fell close to 2% of GDP, and unemployment edged towards 10%. The economy has expanded for thirteen consecutive quarters. Despite recent economic successes, however, the situation is still fragile, but there are good reasons for optimism. Portuguese companies have been successful at diversifying their export markets and investments, increasing the technology content of their exports, and adding value to their products. Yet, Portugal still needs to improve productivity, foster a more flexible economy with a better-educated labour force, achieve higher savings and investment, and develop a more efficient public sector.

---

[35] See Sebastián Royo, 'Crisis and Opportunities in Transition Times', in *Portugal in the Twenty-first Century: Politics, Society and Economics*, ed. by Sebastián Royo (Lanham, MD: Lexington Books, 2011), pp. 1–23.

Portugal's Social and Labour Market Policy: The Crisis, the Troika and Beyond

Miguel Glatzer

La Salle University, Philadelphia, PA

The financial and economic crisis experienced by southern Europe from 2009 to 2014 (ongoing in Greece), and the response to it by national governments and supranational institutions, had profound social, political and policy consequences. Unemployment soared, mass emigration began anew. In depression-ridden Greece, Médecins Sans Frontières opened healthcare facilities for the first time in Western Europe. In many countries, party systems have been upended. New populist parties, on both the right and left, have emerged to challenge long-established parties that now find themselves discredited. Trust in the European Union has declined to lows never seen before in southern Europe and, matched with low levels of trust in national governments, led to growing concern about a broad lack of trust in political institutions.

The crisis led to major debates about its causes. Policy makers and mass publics in northern Europe largely blamed fiscal profligacy in southern Europe, while others found inherent flaws in the design of the euro to be at the root of the problem, with capital flows to southern Europe causing inflated unit labour costs, a shift to the non-tradable sector, and current account deficits. Debates ensued about the wisdom of having entered the euro and the costs (and viability) of leaving it. Ultimately, however, even in the face of deeply unpopular policy prescriptions from the EU, in no country did a majority of the population support leaving the single currency.

The financial and economic crisis that buffeted Portugal and turned into a sovereign debt crisis gave European Union institutions an unprecedented command of social and labour market policy. With the exception of limited domains such as gender equality and occupational health and safety, the EU had long left to the national level the precise determination of social and labour market policy. The open method of coordination could promote discussion and cross-country learning but was soft by design. Although the concept of 'Social Europe' was regarded as an attractive model of society by many (and something to be avoided by others), the EU continued to be characterized by significant national diversity in social protection. Spending levels, institutional structure and programme design, as well as coverage, effectiveness and sustainability vary considerably. Typologies of Bismarckian, social democratic, liberal (and southern European) welfare states remain relevant, even while analysts are quick to point out divergent reform trajectories within these categories. And when convergence did occur, rarely was it at the direct hand of the European Union.

The sovereign debt crises gave unparalleled control of welfare state policy in Portugal to external actors. Facing quickly deteriorating financial conditions and prohibitive interest rates in the bond markets, the Portuguese government signed Memorandums of Understanding (MoUs) with the Troika — the European Commission, the European Central Bank and the IMF. These packages of financial assistance came with strict conditionalities. In social and labour market policy, they were deeply unpopular to many. Seen as eviscerating social rights acquired over a long period of democratic struggle, they led to demonstrations and strikes. Some saw them as illegitimate because they were imposed externally. Others saw them as useful, a *'vincolo esterno'* that could break through logjams and vested interests to enact long-blocked reforms.[1]

This article examines the Troika's effects on labour market policy in Portugal and the recent rollback of some of these measures by the socialist minority government, made possible by (1) the conclusion of the MoU, (2) Portugal's success in reducing its budget deficit, and (3) EU supervision under the European Semester system, which is less constraining than bailout conditionality when countries meet their budget targets (but which can quickly turn harsh when countries do not). A central theme of the article is the changing nature of labour market governance in Portugal, namely from large levels of national autonomy prior to the crisis, to external imposition under bailout conditionality, to a limited rollback of some measures under the António Costa government. The article also covers related elements of pension policy, the minimum wage and anti-poverty programmes. It starts with an overview of the effects of the crisis and policy responses to it on unemployment, poverty, inequality and emigration.

Measuring the Crisis: Negative Economic Growth and Labour Market Dynamics

Portugal's low rates of economic growth upon joining the euro turned negative during the crisis. GDP declined by 3% in 2009, 1.8% in 2011, 4% in 2012 and 1.1% in 2013.[2] By 2015, total GDP was 5.6% lower than in 2008. Portuguese workers became poorer relative to their European counterparts. Using purchasing power parity to control for different prices of the same basket of goods across

---

[1] For the concept of *vincolo esterno* ('external restraint'), see Kenneth Dyson and Kevin Featherstone, 'Italy and EMU as a "Vincolo Esterno": Empowering the Technocrats, Transforming the State', *South European Society and Politics*, 1.2 (1996), 272–99.
[2] Ministério do Trabalho, Solidariedade e Segurança Social, *Livro Verde Sobre as Relações Laborais 2016* (Lisbon: Gabinete de Estratégia e Planeamento do Ministério do Trabalho, Solidariedade e Segurança Social, 2016), p. 46.

countries, the compensation of Portuguese workers fell from 77.9% of the EU 28 average in 2010 to 72.3% in 2015.[3] Unemployment increased from 7.6% in 2008 to a peak of 16.2% in 2013 before falling to 12.4% in 2015.[4] However, broader definitions of unemployment, that include part-time workers who wish to work full-time as well as people discouraged from looking for work, reached a peak of 25.4% in 2013 before falling to 21.3% in 2015.[5] Particular populations suffered disproportionately, among them young people: youth unemployment (among those aged 15 to 24) soared, peaking at 40% in 2013.[6] Another group hit especially hard was the long-term unemployed, who constituted a comparatively large share of those unemployed: 45.8% of the unemployed in 2015 had been unemployed for 25 months or longer, for example.[7] Particularly troubling too was the rise in zero-employment households.

A country of emigration for much of the twentieth century, Portugal had experienced a reversal in recent decades, becoming a net receiver of immigrants, particularly from Brazil, Eastern Europe and some of its former African colonies. As economic conditions deteriorated, many immigrants departed, but alongside them many Portuguese left as well, as the difficulty in finding work led to the resumption of mass emigration. Between 2011 and 2015, 586,000 people in total left the country, a significant minority of whom held university degrees: close to 30% of emigrants in 2015 had completed higher education.[8] From 2008 to 2016, remittances to Portugal increased by 29%, reaching 1.8% of GDP,[9] enabling Portugal to eliminate its current account deficit in 2016. However, it is too early to know the degree to which this Portuguese emigrant stream is temporary or permanent. If permanent, it will reduce human capital in Portugal and exacerbate the ratio of pensioners to workers.

Trends in Inequality and Poverty

Between 2009 and 2014 all deciles experienced a drop in real disposable income (the combined result of the crisis and austerity measures, including cuts in benefits and increases in taxes). However, the drop in income was greatest in the bottom two deciles. While deciles 3 to 7 saw drops of 10% to 12%, and the wealthiest decile a drop in 13%, the bottom decile experienced a 25% fall in income.[10] The S90/S10 indicator, which measures the income ratio of people

[3] Ibid., p. 48.
[4] Ibid., p. 83.
[5] Ibid., p. 91.
[6] Ibid., p. 83.
[7] Ibid., p. 98.
[8] Ibid., p. 67.
[9] Pordata, 'Remittances by emigrants, immigrants and balance as a percentage of GDP', available at <https://www.pordata.pt/en/Portugal/Remittances+by+emigrants++immigrants+and+balance+as+a+percentage+of+GDP-2366> [accessed 26 February 2018].
[10] Carlos Farinha Rodrigues (ed.), Rita Figueira and Vítor Junqueira, *Introdução ao estudo Desigualdade do rendimento e pobreza em Portugal, 2009–2014* (Lisbon: Fundação Francisco Manuel

at the 90th percentile and the 10th, rose from 9.2 to 10.6. The S95/S05 measure increased even more dramatically. A person at the 95th percentile had 14.7 times the income of someone at the 5th percentile in 2009, but had 18.7 times the income in 2014.[11] Given that top incomes declined during this period, Rodrigues, Figueira and Junqueira note that the increase in the ratio is due to an extraordinary contraction of income at the bottom of the income distribution. They find, however, that the principal cause of the widening inequality is changes in market income rather than changes in net social transfers (benefits after taxes).

Using the official European poverty line (income below 60% of median national income), poverty in Portugal increased by 8.8% between 2009 and 2014, leading to an increase in the poverty rate from 17.7% to 19.5%. With this measure, 2,020,000 people were classified as poor in 2014.[12] However, because median income fell during most of this period, the official poverty line also fell, from 434 euros per month in 2009 to 409 euros per month in 2013; it then rose again, along with median incomes, to 422 euros per month in 2014. An anchored poverty rate solves this problem by fixing the poverty line at a particular point in time and adjusting it not for median income but for inflation. Following this procedure, a poverty line of 433 euros in 2009 corresponds to a poverty line of 470 euros in 2014; in other words, a person with 470 euros of income in 2014 would have the same purchasing power as someone with 433 euros had in 2009. Using the anchored poverty line, an additional 500,000 people would qualify as poor. By this measure, a full 24.2% of the population would be classified as poor in 2014.[13]

Poverty was unequally distributed by age group. While those aged 65 and older saw their anchored poverty rate increase from 13.8% in 2010 to 14.6% in 2013, increases were substantially larger among the working-age population of 18 to 64 year olds (from 12.9% to 19.3%) and among the young under 18 years of age (from 12.9% to 19.3%).[14] The unemployed were particularly likely to be poor. In 2012, 40.2% were poor.[15] With a poverty rate of 40.4%, families with three or more children were equally likely to be poor. However, pensioners were much more effectively protected by social transfers than younger groups in the population, reflecting the Bismarckian nature of the Portuguese welfare state (where benefits are strongly correlated to contributions), as well as its elderly bias. This was also the result of budgetary decisions taken during the turn to austerity, under the Memorandums of Understanding, which affected younger people more than the elderly.

---

dos Santos, 2016), p. 13.
[11] Ibid., p. 15.
[12] Ibid., p. 17.
[13] Ibid., p. 19.
[14] José António Pereirinha, 'Pobreza e novos riscos sociais em Portugal: uma análise da despesa social', in *Políticas sociais em tempo de crise: perspectivas, tendências e questões críticas*, ed. by Cristina Albuquerque and Helena Amara da Luz (Lisbon: PACTOR, 2016), pp. 125–44 (p. 128).
[15] OECD, *OECD Economic Surveys: Portugal 2014* (Paris: OECD), p. 94.

From Stimulus to Austerity and Structural Reform under the Troika

In step with most European countries, Portugal's initial reaction to the crisis in early 2009 and 2010 involved an increase in social spending, most of which occurred automatically because more people qualified for existing programmes.[16] Thus, spending on unemployment benefits increased as unemployment grew, as did spending on minimum income programmes such as the Rendimento Social de Inserção as more people fell into deep poverty. Policy changes that increased social spending, such as increases in the duration of unemployment assistance, also occurred in this initial period.

While the European Commission had encouraged this form of stimulus in the face of recession (along with the Obama administration, which continued to argue for a coordinated multilateral stimulus on both sides of the Atlantic), by mid-2010 the Commission had made a dramatic U-turn in its policy stance. Increasingly, the concern lay with controlling budget deficits, and the policy prescription turned to austerity. The Socialist government announced successive Stabilization and Growth Programmes (Programas de Estabilidade e Crescimento, or PECs), which froze pensions and assistance benefits, tightened spending on non-contributory programmes and imposed a special tax on higher pensions, among other measures.

In May 2011, facing a sovereign debt crisis due to increasingly untenable interest rates on its bonds, Portugal accepted a bailout package of 78 billion euros with the European Commission, the European Central Bank and the International Monetary Fund, known colloquially as the Troika. In agreeing to several Memorandums of Understanding (MoUs), Portugal was placed under a regime of conditionality. The MoUs imposed austerity through specific budgetary targets but also required a programme of detailed structural reforms across multiple policy areas. These reforms were to be carried out against a detailed timeline and externally monitored. Portugal remained under the external supervision of the Troika for precisely three years, from May 2011 to May 2014.

The initial expansion in public spending, along with higher interest payments on sovereign debt and the drop in GDP from the recession, produced a dramatic increase in government spending as a percentage of GDP, from under 46% in 2008 to close to 52% at its peak, in 2010.[17] The composition of this spending changed as well. Interest payments on government debt climbed from 2.6% of GDP in 2006 to 2.9% in 2010, and to 4.9% in 2014, dropping slightly to 4.6% in 2015. The public sector wage bill reached a peak of 14.5% of GDP in 2005, and has dropped relatively continuously since then to 11.3% in 2015, due to freezes in wages and promotions as well as layoffs and retirements. Social

---

[16] Ministério do Trabalho, Solidariedade e Segurança Social, *Livro Verde Sobre as Relações Laborais 2016* (Lisbon: Gabinete de Estratégia e Planeamento do Ministério do Trabalho, Solidariedade e Segurança Social, 2016), p. 36.
[17] Ibid., p. 54.

transfers experienced the highest growth, rising from 16% in 2008 to 19.1% in 2015. This was due primarily to the increase in need, stemming from the growth in poverty and unemployment, as well as to population ageing and increases in the number of pensioners. In attempting to control this growth in social spending amid greater need, Portugal altered eligibility rules, payment levels and the length of time benefits could be received.

After an initial decline from 2008 to 2009, government revenue as a proportion of GDP increased substantially, by more than 5 percentage points to reach a peak of 45.1% in 2013, before declining slightly to 44.6% in 2014 and 43.8% in 2015. While part of this growth was due to tax increases in the 2010–13 period, much of it is due to the fall in GDP. The large deficits during the deepest years of the crisis fuelled a ballooning of total government debt to over 130% of GDP in 2014.

Starting in the second semester of 2010, Portugal shifted from a policy of anti-cyclical deficit spending to a stance focused on deficit reduction, a process that was accentuated under the MoUs. For social transfers, the impact occurred primarily through a mix of tax increases and cuts in programme generosity. Child benefits were cut by 32.3% between 2010 and 2012. In the same period the social integration scheme (Rendimento Social de Inserção, RSI) was cut by 28.8% and widows' and widowers' benefits by 7.7%.[18] Initially frozen, pensions were later reduced on a progressive scale and a special solidarity tax implemented on pensions above 5000 euros per month. Payment of the 13th and 14th months' pensions (paid in the summer and at Christmas) was suspended. When the Constitutional Court ruled against a number of Troika-imposed measures on social benefits and labour law in April, August and November 2013, the government plugged part of the resulting shortfall in savings by increasing the retirement age for public employees and levying an additional tax on all pensions over 600 euros.[19]

The wide-ranging programme of structural reforms detailed in the MoUs included a substantial liberalization of labour market regulation and large-scale changes to the workings of the collective bargaining system. Under the easy-to-fire, easy-to-hire theory, high dismissal costs were viewed as contributing to employers' reluctance to hire workers on regular contracts. As a result, the Troika called for a lowering of dismissal costs. Criteria for fair dismissals were widened and severance payments were lowered. While the reduction in employment security for workers on regular work contracts between 2010 and 2013 was considerable, Portugal continued to have high levels relative to other Eurozone countries at the end of this period.[20] This is because most other

---

[18] Luís Bernardo, Manuela Silva and Tiago Correia, 'A saúde pública como investimento social', in *Estado social de todos para todos*, ed. by Renato Miguel do Carmo and André Barata (Lisbon: Tinta da China, 2014), pp. 91–134 (p. 110).
[19] Maria Petmesidou and Miguel Glatzer, 'The Crisis Imperative, Reform Dynamics and Rescaling in Greece and Portugal', *European Journal of Social Security*, 17.2 (2015), 158–81 (p. 167).
[20] Amílcar Moreira, Ángel Alonso Domínguez, Cátia Antunes, Maria Karamessini, Michele Raitano

countries also took measures to liberalize individual and collective dismissals, even when not under Troika conditionality.

In an attempt to reduce high levels of labour market dualism between permanent and fixed-term contracts, reforms made to the latter permitted longer terms and additional extensions, to an 18-month maximum. Labour costs were lowered by freezing the minimum wage, reducing the premium for overtime pay by 50%, ending the 13th and 14th months of pay, and eliminating four public holidays.

To increase the unemployment benefit coverage rate, the contribution period to qualify for benefits was lowered from 15 months to 12. However, the maximum duration of benefits was substantially reduced, from 30 to 18 months. Collective bargaining was dramatically reformed by limiting automatic extension to non-unionized workers. As a result, by 2012 collective agreements covered only 327,600 private sector workers, a steep drop from the 1.9 million covered in 2008. Furthermore, the locus of collective bargaining was increasingly decentralized from the national to the firm level. The combined effect of external imposition of measures in social policy and labour law, and decentralization of collective agreements, was a hollowing out of social dialogue: tripartite institutions, where government, labour unions and employer federations met to discuss and agree on policy reforms, continued to exist but their ability to shape policy was severely constrained.[21]

Reversing the Damage? Policy Reforms after the Troika and under the European Semester

The legislative elections of 4 October 2015 produced a hung parliament. Controversially, President Cavaco Silva invited Prime Minister Pedro Passos Coelho to form a minority government when the Portugal Ahead alliance between his Social Democrats and the Popular Party emerged as the largest bloc in parliament, but without an absolute majority. António Costa, leader of the Socialists, argued that his party, supported by parties to its left, could produce a government with greater support in parliament. The minority government of Pedro Passos Coelho lasted less than two weeks, falling when the Socialists voted against its government programme. Appointed Prime Minister on 24 November 2015, António Costa was able to form a minority government with the support of the Left Bloc, the Greens and the Communist Party.

By the end of 2015, then, Portugal found itself in a new situation. No longer under the conditionality of the Troika (which had ended in May 2014 due to the resumption of economic growth and reduction in structural deficits), it now had a Socialist government whose programme differed from that of the

and Miguel Glatzer, 'Austerity-Driven Labour Market Reforms in Southern Europe: Eroding the Security of Labour Market Insiders', *European Journal of Social Security*, 17.2 (2015), 202–25 (p. 219).

[21] Maria Petmesidou and Miguel Glatzer, 'The Crisis Imperative', p. 173.

outgoing Social Democrats. Under such circumstances, would the government be able to change course in social and labour market policy?

The departure from formal Troika control did not mean the end of European supervision, however. Beginning in 2010 and 2011, as the crisis intensified, and continuing since, the EU engaged in a robust debate regarding how to adapt its institutional architecture in the face of shocks that were often asymmetric, affecting some countries more than others. Proposals that involved greater risk-sharing, such as for Eurobonds, were routinely rejected by Germany. Others, however, that involved greater supervision of national budgets by European institutions, thus reinforcing the Growth and Stability Pact, were approved. This was the case with the Six-Pack (adopted in 2011), the Fiscal Compact (adopted in 2012), and the Two-Pack (added in 2013). Collectively these instruments increased EU monitoring of national debt and budget deficits, requiring submission of a wider number of indicators, evidence of progress towards Medium-Term Objectives, and prior oversight of Draft Budgetary Plans. They facilitate and, in some cases, mandate the launching of corrective action through processes such as Alert Mechanism Reports, the Macroeconomic Imbalance Procedure, or revisions of Draft Budgetary Plans. They also strengthen penalties for non-compliance through Excessive Deficit Procedures and sanctions that require Reverse Qualified Majority Voting in the Economic and Financial Affairs Council (ECOFIN) to overturn, thus boosting the power of the Commission, in particular its Directorate-General for Economic and Financial Affairs (DG ECFIN). A review of these instruments designed to strengthen budgetary discipline and fiscal consolidation scored them as uniformly high in the external pressure they place on a country's policy aims and their powers of surveillance, and mostly high in their enforcement capacities.[22] By contrast, instruments adopted during the crisis to promote coordination of social and labour market policy, including the upgrading of skills, the improvement of working conditions and job quality and the reduction of poverty, are scored as having mostly modest (and thus non-intrusive) policy objectives and relatively weak levels of surveillance and enforcement. This is the case with Europe 2020, unveiled in 2010 and which replaces the Lisbon Strategy; the Euro-Plus Pact of 2011; and the Social Investment Package and Youth Guarantee, announced in 2013.[23]

For these instruments, the principal monitoring system is the European Semester. This annual process encompasses both budgetary policy, which covers stability and convergence programmes, and economic policy, which includes employment and social policy among others.[24] Portugal, like most EU

---

[22] Caroline de la Porte and Elke Heins, 'A New Era of European Integration? Governance of Labour Market and Social Policy since the Sovereign Debt Crisis', *Comparative European Politics*, 13 (2015), 8–28 (p. 23).
[23] Ibid., p. 23.
[24] For an overview of the European semester, as well as a portal to many documents, please see the European Semester's website: <http://www.consilium.europa.eu/en/policies/european-semester/>.

member states, has been part of the process since 2014 and has now received annual recommendations for four years.

Because the current Socialist government took office under improving economic conditions, with increasing employment, a return to growth and a continued increase in exports fuelled by wider Eurozone growth, it has been able to present a decent record on macroeconomic issues and the budget deficit. A recent monitoring report noted Portugal's 'plausible' projections on deficit controls for 2017 while expressing caution for 2018 and beyond, as well as concern about Portugal's continued high debt levels and the continuing need for measures to support banks.[25] As a result, Portugal has had at least limited leeway to reverse some of the austerity measures imposed during the crisis, and this is what the Socialist government has done.

In the words of José António Vieira da Silva, Portugal's current Minister of Employment, Solidarity and Social Security, 'between 2011 and 2015 Portugal went through a process of deep deregulation and, especially, individualization of labour relations, at the expense of social dialogue, collective contracts and balanced labour relations, which led to a significant expansion of precariousness.'[26] Mindful of the need to keep budgetary deficits below 3%, the government took steps that partially roll back the deregulatory and austerity measures of the Troika years.

In January 2016, following an agreement with the employer federations and the UGT union, the government raised the minimum wage from 505 euros to 530 euros. Because the agreement included a reduction of 0.75% in social security contributions paid by employers for workers earning up to or below 530 euros, the Confederation of Portuguese Workers (CGTP) declined to sign it.[27] Under the PSD government it had been frozen at 485 euros from 2011 to October 2014, when the centre-right government raised it to 505. While voting against a proposal to raise the minimum wage to 600 euros introduced by the Portuguese Communist Party in late 2016, the Socialists called for gradual annual increases that would allow the minimum wage to reach this level in 2019. In 2017, the minimum wage was increased again, to 557 euros. To reduce the impact on employers, the increase was combined with a 1.25% reduction in their social security contributions, leading the CGTP to reject this tripartite agreement as well. As of March 2017, 730,000 workers, representing 22.9% of employed, earned this statutory minimum.[28]

[25] European Commission, *Recommendation for a Council Recommendation on the 2017 National Reform Programme of Portugal and delivering a Council opinion on the 2017 Stability Programme of Portugal* (Brussels, 22 May 2017) COM(2017) 521 final, p. 4.
[26] José António Vieira da Silva, *Livro Verde Sobre as Relações Laborais 2016* (Lisbon: Gabinete de Estratégia e Planeamento do Ministério do Trabalho, Solidariedade e Segurança Social, 2016), p. 24.
[27] Eurofound, 'Portugal: Developments in Working Life — Q1 2016', 13 May 2016. Online at <https://www.eurofound.europa.eu/observatories/eurwork/articles/working-conditions/portugal-developments-in-working-life-q1-2016>.
[28] The Portugal News/Lusa, 'Minimum salary applied to 730,000 workers in March, 23% of workforce', 4 June 2017. Online at <http://www.theportugalnews.com/news/minimum-salary-applied-

In the first months of its term, the government took additional steps to reverse some of the austerity measures affecting social transfers, particularly though not exclusively on programmes affecting the poor. The measures covered retirement pensions, the solidarity supplement for the elderly (which boosts pensions that are particularly low), the social integration scheme (Rendimento Social de Inserção, RSI) paid to families with very low incomes, and family allowances (Abono de Família). The four public holidays that the previous government had eliminated were also restored.

Notably, the government undertook these measures during a period when labour market trends were negative. Unemployment rose from 11.9% to 12.2% from the fourth quarter of 2015 to the first quarter of 2016, temporary employment continued to grow and the percentage of workers earning the minimum wage rose substantially. While these trends indicated the need for additional concern with issues of poverty and need, they also produced pressure on the government budget, through decreased tax revenue and increased expenditure on programmes such as unemployment benefits.

By the third quarter of 2016, macroeconomic trends and labour market indicators had turned positive. Unemployment dropped from 12.4% in the second quarter to 10.8% in the third, and the household savings rate stopped falling. Compared to the first six months of 2015, business investment in industry and manufacturing in the first half of 2016 was up by 70% and 60%, respectively, and positive trends in EU-wide employment indicated that exports were likely to rise.[29] Crucially, the late September estimate for the 2016 budget deficit stood at 2.5%, the lowest since 1999. This provided room for the government to further reverse some of the austerity measures of the Troika years while still meeting the budgetary targets of the Growth and Stability Pact and the monitoring requirements of the European Semester.

In May 2017 the government loosened restrictions on unemployment assistance that had been introduced in 2012 as part of the MoU with the Troika. The new rule eliminates the 10% reduction in unemployment assistance (the social protection in unemployment regime) after 180 days for benefits of 421.32 euros, the equivalent of the Social Support Index (IAS). The new rule also sets the IAS as the floor for this unemployment benefit. This Decree-Law was criticized for not going far enough by the CGTP, which demanded the complete removal of the 10% penalty and argued that the minimum level of social protection was still too low.

In August 2017, the penalty for early retirement was eliminated for workers aged 60 and above who had paid contributions for 48 years or more and to those who started work before the age of 15 and had paid contributions for 46 years or more. The Prime Minister argued that fairness demanded that those who

---

to-730000-workers-in-march-23-of-workforce/42146>.
[29] Eurofound, 'Portugal: Latest Working Life Developments — Q3 2016', 28 October 2016. Online at <https://www.eurofound.europa.eu/observatories/eurwork/articles/working-conditions-industrial-relations/portugal-latest-working-life-developments-q3–2016>.

started work at 14 or younger and had long contributory careers be permitted to retire at age 60 without penalty, saying that he was 'righting the injustice that was worsened in recent years, with the double penalizing effect of the increase in the retirement age and the worsening of the sustainability factor that rose from 5.4 percent to 12.3 percent'.[30]

In part because public sector workers had been hit hard by austerity measures under the Troika and in part because the public sector is an important source of votes for the Socialists, the government also took several steps to improve working conditions for public sector workers. An early measure restored the public sector's 35-hour working week. While no wage increases were expected in 2017, the 2017 budget provided for the resumption of career progression, frozen since 2011.

It also included provisions to reduce precarious employment in the public sector, regularizing contracts and reducing the use of temporary work contracts and subcontracting. Under pressure from an association calling itself the State Precariate (Precários do Estado), the government announced a process whereby each case of a precarious contract will be evaluated to see if it matches permanent staff needs and corresponds to full-time functions in public administration. Public sector trade unions are given a role in this process.

The regime of requalification for civil servants whose roles had been lost in administrative restructuring was also reformed. Under the previous regime, also a product of the MoU with the Troika, workers in this situation faced a 40% cut in wages in the first year and a 60% cut in subsequent years, with the possibility of dismissal. The new regime ends these measures and instead emphasizes training and reskilling.[31]

Additional initiatives in the field of social and labour market policy include the launching of QUALIFICA, a new programme of professional training and adult education, with certification of competencies. Despite substantial increases in the proportion of young adults with university degrees, Portugal's labour force remains heavily under-schooled and under-trained by European standards. Reducing this gap has been a priority for many years and the policy is in line with the social investment approach of recent EU policy advice as well as OECD recommendations to Portugal to focus on active labour market policy. Portugal's National Reform Programme, submitted as part of its compliance with the European Semester, emphasizes this commitment to a structural upgrading of labour force skills.

---

[30] The Portugal News/Lusa, 'Early-retirement penalty for long-serving workers to go in August', 20 April 2017. Online at <http://theportugalnews.com/news/early-retirement-penalty-for-long-serving-workers-to-go-in-august/41732>. Sustainability factors use measures of increased life expectancy at retirement to improve the financial resilience of pension systems. Increased life expectancy results in downward adjustments to pension levels.
[31] Eurofound, 'Portugal: Latest Working Life Developments — Q2 2017', 31 July 2017. Online at <https://www.eurofound.europa.eu/observatories/eurwork/articles/portugal-latest-working-life-developments-q2-2017>.

Also of note are proposals to address gender inequality in the labour market. One measure would increase gender balance in management and supervisory bodies in public sector companies and listed firms. Under this proposal, neither gender would be able to fall below 33.3% of corporate decision-making bodies, though the private sector would have an additional two years (until 1 January 2020) to meet this target. Also being developed are proposed measures on parental rights and the gender pay gap. While these requirements would have virtually no budgetary impact, they are an example of progressive policy-making that attempts to reduce inequities and inequality.

As already suggested, a restoration of collective bargaining and dialogue with the social partners has been an important goal. Many of the measures detailed above emerged after consultation with employer federations and labour unions. A large number of collective bargaining agreements in the public sector, mostly between unions and municipal governments, came into force. Many of these had been signed prior to the Socialist government taking office but had been suspended by the previous government. A Constitutional Court decision found the suspension unconstitutional. The first months of 2016 also saw a rise of 17.7% in collective agreements in the private sector, with growth of 21.3% in the number of workers covered, but the share of workers covered still remained far below the level of 2011, when the automatic extension of collective agreements was deeply restricted.[32] In May 2017, a Resolution was issued that repealed restrictions on collective bargaining imposed in 2012 and 2014 as part of the MoU agreement between the previous government and the Troika. The new resolution facilitates the extension of collective agreements by setting a short timeframe of 35 days for analysis, public consultation and announcement of extension orders, and creates a new body in the Ministry of Labour to implement the process. Collective agreements are now designed to promote social and gender equality by using as criteria their effect in reducing wage inequality and by examining their effect on women.[33]

The constraining capabilities of the European Semester programme, along with the lag inherent in its procedural calendar, were evident in the summer of 2016. On 12 July 2016, the Economic and Financial Affairs Council of the European Union (ECOFIN) opened a process to sanction Portugal for excessive deficits in 2015. While the European Commission subsequently recommended a suspension of the fine, it held open the possibility of partially withholding structural funds, to be decided in September. With the exception of the CGTP, Portugal's social partners issued a joint statement urging ECOFIN to adopt the Commission's recommendation. The statement stressed the 'enormous

---

[32] Eurofound, 'Portugal: Latest Working Life Developments — Q2 2016', 5 August 2016. Online at <https://www.eurofound.europa.eu/observatories/eurwork/articles/working-conditions-labour-market-industrial-relations-law-and-regulation/portugal-latest-working-life-developments-q2-2016>.
[33] Eurofound, 'Portugal: Latest Working Life Developments — Q2 2017', 31 July 2017. Online at <https://www.eurofound.europa.eu/observatories/eurwork/articles/portugal-latest-working-life-developments-q2-2017>.

contribution to fiscal consolidation' Portugal had made in recent years and argued that financial and fiscal policies needed to be reconciled with growth and stabilization policies.[34] Calling structural funds 'an important lever for investment' and 'an essential and central source' for Portugal's modernization, particularly in the face of constraints on national public investment, the partners described the proposed suspension as 'deeply unfair and counterproductive'.[35] While the CGTP did not sign the statement, it criticized the European Semester process in harsh terms arguing that 'the European Commission's decision to apply a "suspended sentence" is an unacceptable measure, aggravated by keeping the country as a hostage by conditioning access to structural funds, at a time when the investment is fundamental to the growth of the economy.'[36]

Conclusion

Portugal's post-Troika experience under a Socialist government allows a number of observations to be drawn regarding the design of social and labour market policy in the wake of austerity and deregulation. First, the Socialists have been deeply fortunate in having their term in office coincide with a period of economic growth. This has provided budgetary space for the repeal of a sizeable number of austerity measures while continuing to make progress in controlling the deficit.

Second, to strike an acceptable balance between the need for budgetary control and the desire to move in a progressive direction, reversals of austerity measures have in general been limited to those with the greatest impact on the poor and the vulnerable. The public sector is a good example of this. Although career progression has resumed and the problem of precarious contracts within the state has been the focus of attention, wages remain frozen. Similarly, unemployment assistance has been modestly reformed by the removal of the 10% penalty after 180 days of benefit, but only for those receiving a low level of benefit. The lowest benefit has also been upgraded to the level of the Social Support Index. Penalties for early retirement have been eliminated for those with many years of contributions who started work at a young age, but for most workers increases in the retirement age and the effect of the life expectancy sustainability factor (see footnote 30) continue to be important.

Third, it is possible to rebuild a system of tripartite bargaining that had been largely marginalized during the imposition of austerity measures detailed

---

[34] General Union of Workers (UGT), Confederation of Portuguese Industry (CIP), Confederation of Portuguese Commerce (CCP), Confederation of Portuguese Farmers (CAP), Portuguese Confederation of Tourism (CTP), 'Common Position Regarding the Non-Application of a Fine and the Partial Suspension of EU Funds to Portugal', UGT, 27 July 2016, p. 1.
[35] Ibid., p. 2.
[36] Quoted in Eurofound, 'Portugal: Latest Working Life Developments — Q3 2016', 28 October 2016. Online at <https://www.eurofound.europa.eu/observatories/eurwork/articles/working-conditions-industrial-relations/portugal-latest-working-life-developments-q3–2016>.

by the Troika and pushed by the previous government. The institutional actors remain the same and the patterns of agreement have reverted to form, with the UGT joining in agreement and the CGTP generally choosing not to sign. Nonetheless, national strikes called by the CGTP have been few and the Communist Party has upheld its commitment to government stability, even when it criticizes progress, such as the upgrading of the minimum wage, as too slow.

Fourth, the reinforced system of EU monitoring embodied in the European Semester has the capacity to constrain member states' social and labour market policy. Through its strong surveillance mechanisms on budgetary deficits and fiscal consolidation and its powerful sanction regime of fines and suspension of structural funds, ECOFIN and the Commission have more tools at their disposal to direct states than was the case before the crisis. The calendar which the European Semester follows is a two-edged sword. On the one hand, it raises the possibility of states being punished for deficits run up in a previous year (as in the 2016 threat to sanction Portugal for deficits incurred in 2015). On the other, it allows for the possibility that subsequent positive performance will obviate the need to take action. Nonetheless, it is seems clear that stimulus in the face of recession, or even social support to needy populations using automatic stabilizers in the face of a recession, is under serious threat if a member state's budget performance is close to the prescribed maximums. The pro-cyclical bias of the Eurozone rules is a particular challenge for countries like Portugal that are constrained by high levels of debt and particularly vulnerable to changes in export markets.

Comparisons to states in the US federal system are instructive. With the European Union budget being small relative to that of the US federal government and with high political resistance to collective measures such as transfers between states or Eurobonds, EU member states with high levels of debt find themselves in an unenviable position. Barred from using budget deficits, they nonetheless lack the rescue role played by the federal government in the US, where transfers from Washington through old-age and disability programmes, Medicare and Medicaid's coverage of health care costs, and food security schemes bring substantial resources to states. Crucially, those transfers rise automatically when need in a state grows, with resulting increases in the number of people electing to retire or qualifying for disability and food assistance. No equivalent mechanism exists in Brussels.

Portugal's ability to use social and labour market policy to cushion the next crisis is thus highly limited. The progressive gains made in reversing austerity measures in these domains by the Socialist government are therefore quite vulnerable to the next economic shock, particularly as other areas of spending (such as public investment) remain constrained.

Portugal's challenges in the social and labour market fields remain high. Chief among them, perhaps, are high rates of inequality and poverty, the continued increase in precarious jobs, and continued skill deficits. Nonetheless, by reversing many of the austerity measures imposed under the Troika years and targeting increases in expenditure on some of the most vulnerable groups, the Socialist government has so far been able to move in a progressive direction.

Reviews

LISA VOIGT, *Spectacular Wealth: The Festivals of Colonial South American Mining Towns* (Austin: University of Texas Press, 2016). 237 pages, 5 b/w photos. Print and e-book. Hardcover and paperback.

Reviewed by BARBARA ALGE (Goethe University, Frankfurt)

Public festivals have had an important function in promoting imperial expansion since the beginning of the colonization of the Americas. They were used to commemorate religious and political events, from important Catholic feast days to political acts such as the entrance of important authorities into colonial towns or weddings of the court. *Spectacular Wealth*, written by Lisa Voigt, complements the vast literature on festivals in eighteenth-century mining towns in colonial South America. While Voigt cites this literature, the novelty of her *Spectacular Wealth* lies, first, in the 'mining' (p. 8) of festival accounts, and, second, in the comparative approach — not only looking at festivals in Spanish and Portuguese America side-by-side, but also working out links, similarities and differences between these two regions.

Drawing on archival research, Voigt examines festival accounts and the festive participation of diverse inhabitants in the silver-mining town of Potosí (viceroyalty of Peru) and in the gold-mining towns of Minas Gerais (Brazil). She not only bridges written texts and performances, but brings the festivals to life by giving a voice to different ethnic and social groups involved in the organization and performance of the festivals, as well as to those writing about the festivals in mining boomtowns, mostly for a metropolitan readership.

While the festivals served the Church and the Crown for ostentation in the first instance, they also offered an opportunity to Amerindians, Afro-descendants, Europeans and creoles to display their social capital and cultural practices in spectacular performances. Festivals were used to redefine the reputation of these groups, and to celebrate their cultural, spiritual and intellectual wealth. Tracing the multiple meanings and messages of civic festivals and religious feast days, Voigt highlights the conflicting agendas at work in the organization, performance and reporting of festivals.

The book is divided by theme and approach rather than geography and corpus: Part I analyses and interprets specific texts on festivals in the Villa Imperial de Potosí (Chapter 1) and on festivals in colonial Minas Gerais (Chapter 2); Part II uses those and other texts to take a closer look at the celebrants of the festivals, with a focus on the natives in Potosí (Chapter 3), and on Afro-Brazilians in Minas Gerais (Chapter 4). Each chapter finishes with a helpful summary of the main points. Extensive notes, well indicated in relation to pages, complement the information given in each chapter and five figures in black-and-white reproduced from eighteenth-century paintings and manuscripts illustrate Voigt's observations. A conclusion tops off the complex narrative.

In the introduction, Voigt presents a description of the play of the *Real tragicomedia del descubrimiento y conquista del Oriente*, performed at a Jesuit college in Lisbon in 1619, to outline the main themes of the book, that is, 'the festive display of mineral wealth; of the feats and fruits of evangelization; of royal authority and ethnic difference, both feigned and real; of intergroup competition and rivalry (again, both feigned and real)' (p. 11). The description of this play by Mimoso (Lisbon, 1620) serves as an example of what Voigt calls the 'ambiguous genre' of festival accounts, lying between the narrative of a performed event and their own rhetorical performances, and as such derived from other texts and oral accounts as well as the performance itself. The introduction further contextualizes the silver rush in Potosí and the gold rush in Minas Gerais historically, and provides insights into the social make-up of the mining towns, composed of those who profited from the minerals, and those who suffered from exploitation working in the mines. Voigt also mentions the writers in Portuguese and Spanish America, who play a role throughout the book, such as Bartolomé Arzáns de Orsúa and Andre João Antonil. She turns her attention to the physical and symbolical presence of different racial and ethnic groups in the festival performances.

Chapter 1 focuses on three festive occasions that Arzáns uses to showcase creole abilities and merit in Potosí: the 1608 Corpus Christi celebrations, the 1622 commemoration of the death of Philip III and the coronation of Philip IV, and the 1716 solemn entry of Archbishop-Viceroy Diego Morcillo Rubio y Auñón. Chapter 2 presents the texts of the *Triunfo Eucharistico* (by Simão Ferreira Machado, 1734) and the *Aureo Throno Episcopal* (anonymous, 1749), describing the festivities around the transfer of the Eucharist to a new parish church in the town of Vila Rica (today Ouro Preto) and the entry of the bishop into the newly created diocese of Mariana. In Chapter 3, Voigt considers the ambivalence with which Spanish and creole authorities viewed indigenous festive participation in Potosí, using Fernangil's *El Dios Pan* and Arzáns' *Historia de la Villa Imperial*. The latter exemplifies the ways in which subordinate groups borrowed, reinterpreted and altered the goals of Spanish and Christian celebrations. The last chapter returns to the texts presented in Chapter 2, working out how members of a Black Brotherhood used the medium of print as a means of self-promotion. The foregrounding of Afro-Brazilian celebrants in the realms of both the repertoire and the archive, performance and print, is an innovative feature of this book.

Overall, the book is a well-constructed and complex narrative, and its introduction a great pleasure to read. Only the information in the main chapters becomes in some parts — due to the difficulty of the material presented — slightly repetitive. The interweaving of Spanish and Portuguese original excerpts in the narrative is a recommendable methodological model. Together with the English translations following each Spanish or Portuguese text, however, the thread of the respective paragraph sometimes loosens up. Having worked on festivals in Minas Gerais myself, I dare to say that Lisa Voigt might have taken some secondary sources too much for granted. To give just one example: stating that the Guerra dos Emboabas in Minas Gerais was a civil war (p. 58) is not incontrovertible, judging from the literature. Furthermore, I miss a discussion of the relation between skin colour and the proximity to slavery in the Brazilian case, or a more diversified view on the issue of class.

Spectacular Wealth is not only of interest to those working on colonial festivals in South America, but is a valuable source for historians, anthropologists, sociologists, theatrologists, musicologists and others working on phenomena resulting from Spanish and Portuguese colonization. Voigt has succeeded in bringing together first-hand eighteenth-century festival accounts with secondary sources and theories on diverse aspects of culture in colonial South America into a seamless narrative.

FRANCINE FERNANDES WEISS RICIERI, *Imagens do Poético em Alphonsus de Guimaraens* (São Paulo: Editora FAP-UNIFESP/EDUSP, 2014), 264 pages. Print.

Reviewed by RAFAEL MENDES, Universidade Federal do Rio de Janeiro

The lyrical writing of Alphonsus de Guimaraens (1870–1921) is rich in expansive possibilities: of the senses, of realities, of perceptions — of possibilities, in sum. His poetic universe is full of vague implications and subtle clarities and is governed by a complex, multifaceted subjectivity that transits between the suggestiveness of his dream-universe and the edge of insanity. Any critical study of his work requires, therefore, a painstaking effort of discursive materialization. Yet this task also requires a structure that accords with the poet's work, in order that there be no conflict or disagreement between poetry and critique (the latter also an art). In our condition as readers, we can recognize that the talent and the astuteness of Francine F. W. Ricieri, a postdoctoral researcher in Brazilian Literature at Unicamp, succeed on both counts, giving us a work of literary criticism that is both ample and precise.

A Brazilian exponent of symbolist aesthetics (together with his peer Cruz e Sousa), Alphonsus de Guimaraens is traditionally read in association with the poetry of Paul Verlaine, one of his overt influences. It is not rare for the poet to mention the loss of his fiancée, still a teenager when she died, this loss being a fundamental theme of a considerable part of his poetic production. The poet's biography and the influence of Verlaine are part of the first problematics Ricieri presents in her study.

Seeking to expand the appreciation of the poet's work, normally limited to a few select themes such as musicality, religiosity, mysticism and its confessional character, Ricieri addresses not only the poet's verse but also his prose writings, which, she believes, reveals the 'multiplicidade de uma escrita até então apreciada como uniforme' [multiplicity of a writing hitherto considered uniform] (p. 19), showing, for example, a hitherto unrecognized humour. In this way Ricieri's critique explores the epigraph from French philosopher Gaston Bachelard with which it shrewdly begins: 'On ne fait pas de poésie au sein d'une unité: l'unique n'a pas de propriété poétique' [We do not write poetry if we are confined to a single note, for the single note has no poetic property]. It is important to mention this French thinker because his critical method inspires Ricieri's own work, which, following his example, explores the duplicities and ambivalences to be found in Alphonsus de Guimaraens's writing.

After a brief but dense recapitulation of the most important elements in the poet's critical reception, the author dedicates herself to discussing, not the biographical elements already exhausted elsewhere, but the 'dinâmica das imagens poéticas' [dynamic of poetic images] forged by the poet (p. 41). This project constitutes the following five chapters of her work.

In the first chapter, for example, 'Dois objetos soturnos' [Two gloomy objects], Ricieri highlights the dubious and saturnine presences of the inkpot and the pipe that appear in the poems 'A cabeça de corvo' [The raven's head] and 'O cachimbo' [The pipe] in the collection *Kyriale*. Though published in 1902, *Kyriale* was written between 1891 and 1895. It would have been the poet's first published book, but he gave up on it, only making his debut as a writer in 1899. It is a book that sparkles with the poetic tension of opposites, which, as in Bachelard, is represented metonymically in Ricieri's analysis by the glass inkpot shaped like a raven's head and the pipe shaped like a skull, which she relates to the poet's 'macabre materialization', one of the concepts devised by the author to approach such poetic objects. Through the suggestive dream-air of this poem, the symbolism of the raven — which here recalls the Raven of Poe, of whom Alphonsus was a reader — and of the skull transfigures these objects in the perception and expression of the poetic subject. The raven seems to supply the poet with the black blood with which he will paint 'versos próprios de um louco' [verses fit for a madman] (Guimaraens *apud* Ricieri, p. 60); the pipe recalls the feminine figure with which the poetic subject dialogues, ironically comparing its beauty to the skull which carries inside itself a 'fogo em brasa' [glowing coals] (Guimaraens *apud* Ricieri, p. 66), which evokes the concept of 'erotismo tanático' [thanatical eroticism] (*ibidem*) coined by scholars of the poet's work. Such hallucinatory images are an important part of Alphonsus de Guimaraens's *oeuvre*. These are some of the most emblematic compositions by Alphonsus, authoritatively analysed by Ricieri, but others are highlighted in the following chapters.

In the second chapter, entitled 'Violando desertos' [Violating deserts], transgressive images of the sacred and the profane are explored through the feminine.

Chapter 3, 'As várias faces de Ismália' [The several faces of Ismália], is a detailed and attentive philological investigation of the trajectory of Alphonsus's most famous poem, which was originally entitled 'Ophelia' but had its title changed to avoid reference to Shakespeare's character. Here Ricieri questions whether the image of Ophelia is not more densely evoked by its very deletion. Chapter 4, entitled 'O salto empalhado' [The stuffed jump], opposes images of paralysis with the poet's frequent evocations of dynamism, of highness and lowness, and of the hell and spring of Persephone. Chapter 5. 'A ave no busto: à guisa de conclusão' [The bird on the bust: by way of conclusion] is the culmination of Ricieri's study, where she highlights the 'encaixe sucessivo e constante de imagens' [successive and constant fitting of images] (p. 218) which maintains a dynamic tension throughout the whole body of Guimaraens's work, which functions as a cycle full of resumptions. Here Ricieiri discusses the image of a static bird that occurs in both Poe and Alphonsus.

With canonical poets such as Guimaraens, it is not easy to add something new to critical debate. Here I must say that Ricieri's work, which is based on her doctoral thesis, is both fluent and weighty, a true success. We may perhaps never see another work on Alphonsus of equal quality.

CELSA PINTO, *Anatomy of a Colonial Capital: Panjim* (Saligão, India: Goa 1556, 2016), 206 pages. Print.

CELSA PINTO, *Colonial Panjim: Its Governance, its People* (Saligão, India: Goa 1556, 2016), 349 pages. Print.

Reviewed by PAUL MELO E CASTRO, University of Leeds

Across the archipelago of the so-called Portuguese-speaking world are a series of urban spaces — from Lisbon to Salvador, Bissau to Luanda, Maputo to Macau — that share certain urban forms rooted in Portuguese colonialism yet differ vastly due to their geographical, economic and anthropological emplacements. Relatively little known among their number is Panjim, the erstwhile capital of the former *Estado da Índia Portuguesa*. In two recent works, the Goan historian Celsa Pinto furnishes us with an informative physical, social and political account of the city based on a thorough sifting of colonial governmental publications. Together her two books offer much to scholars conducting research on Indo-Portuguese culture and history and those interested in a comparative understanding of lusotopic urbanism, particular against the backdrop of other imperial city morphologies and social formations, though such comparative analysis is not part of Pinto's objectives.

In *Anatomy of a Colonial Capital: Panjim,* Pinto focuses on the physical transformation of the city, specifically acquisition of land, landfill and the progressive development of the urban structure of the city between 1843 — when the capital of the *Estado* was transferred to Nova Goa, of which modern-day Panjim was part — and 1961, the end of colonial rule and the beginning of a sea change in municipal development and civic outlook. As befits the title, this volume is an essentially empirical account narrating the spatial evolution of Panjim, with only incidental attention given to its development as a *place*, a space endowed with human symbolism and importance, and the political tussles and social wrangling this process doubtless involved. Some personal initiatives and individual acts of resistance to developments are mentioned, but not analysed as part of the struggle of competing interests in Panjim, outside a rather flattened idea of colonizer versus colonized. More maps and visual aids, perhaps at the beginning of each chapter, showing the precise locales and edifices under discussion, would have greatly enhanced Pinto's account (though probably also dilated the book's production costs and cover price). There is an appendix listing the roads of the city for 1903 but little indication of how these map onto the current names (many of which were changed subsequent to the ousting of the Portuguese). Nonetheless, for a student of literature such as myself the various spaces that Pinto indexes and describes provide a treasure-trove of references to decipher the realia of Goan literary works, especially those from the late nineteenth and early twentieth centuries. Readers wishing to picture spaces such as the Navegação Fluvial, a recurrent locale in early twentieth-century fiction, will find much to stimulate their mind's eye.

In the companion volume *Colonial Panjim: Its Governance, its People*, Pinto moves past the data-gathering of her first book to focus, though still with an empirical bent, on the human element of the urban scene. Again it provides valuable — and concisely presented — insights for the English-language reader into the fine-grained texture of the past. This ranges from tables explaining the conversions between the various systems of currency, weights and measures (native, British and Portuguese) to the institutional structures of local colonial government. Pinto's attention to the workaday city activities in the nineteenth and twentieth centuries both enriches our understanding and allows us to see how certain problems of the current day are continuations of old issues, only exacerbated by population growth and the durability of modern discardable materials.

Various fascinating details from the past float up in Pinto's narrative, such as the proposal in 1863 that — given that the Bongis brought in from British India for the task were not performing it satisfactorily — one hundred 'blacks from Angola' be shipped in to deal with the night soil produced by the city, a plan that ultimately appears to have been shelved for lack of funds. Other details provide some insight into the oddments of everyday life, such as the information that, in 1902, the increasing popularity of bicycles prompted the drawing-up of official regulations governing their use. According to these regulations, the owners of dogs, which often attacked cyclists — a new and strange sight we can only presume — were compelled to control their animals or face legal punishment. On occasion the bare facts Pinto digs up from long expired rules and regulations have the quality of a sad short story, such as the record that in 1930, at the Hindu Crematorium in Gaspar Dias, to have a child under seven cremated would have cost the lower-caste bereaved a single rupee. In line with the empirical approach taken by the author, such details are not interpreted or worked up into theses on the society of the time, but rather allowed to resonate for the reader insofar as his or her pre-existing contextual understanding permits.

If there is a criticism to be made here it concerns the uneven chronological coverage: most of the material Pinto relays is from the period around the 1870s. After the first decade of the twentieth century, when Panjim still had more than half a century ahead of it as a colonial city, her account dwindles away to nothing. If this timeframe was determined by choice, then, duly justified, Pinto's book would have been better titled *Colonial Panjim in the Nineteenth Century*. If her focus reflects the limited availability of documentation from the twentieth century, then this major historiographical issue surely requires discussion in the introduction. Nevertheless, despite the unevenness of its scope, Pinto's work remains a compendium of fascinating facts that greatly enriches our sense of the past in the *Estado da Índia*.

One final remark: as with most recent Indian publications in English regarding Goan colonial history, Pinto's two books show some inconsistency — not to say inaccuracy, though far less so than compared to other parallel works — in the spelling of Portuguese words. This inconsistency is in part due to the various spelling reforms the period studied covers (and the fact that, due to the shift to English, Portuguese in Goa is an archival language stuck in the past). Just what the right solution to adopt might be is open to debate, though certainly it is an issue that needs at least some prefatory comment.

LEOPOLDO DA ROCHA, *Cruz de Guerra e outros textos* (Vila do Conde: Adab Edições, 2017), 213 pages. Print.

Reviewed by CIELO G. FESTINO, Paulista University, Pensando Goa, FAPESP

Leopoldo da Rocha is a Goan writer who moved to Lisbon some years after India's takeover of Goa in 1961. His latest book, *Cruz de Guerra e outros textos* [*War Cross and Other Texts*] is a collection of short stories, biographical portraits, anecdotes, pieces of literary criticism and brief historical accounts in the Portuguese language. Rocha himself is a protean figure who dons different masks as he moves from one story to the next to keep the narrative flowing. He is Leopoldo for an interview with a Portuguese academic journal; he adopts the alter ego Menezes in some of the short stories, while in others, together with his wife and his sister, the Goan writer Maria Elsa da Rocha, he becomes a secondary character; in nineteenth-century fashion, he addresses his reader directly as '*meu amável leitor*' [my kind reader]; he is on first-name terms with some of the Goan historical figures presented in his narratives and rarely tells stories from hearsay but, rather, from personal experience.

If Rocha's narrative skills, as shown in the short stories compiled in *Cruz de Guerra e outros textos* [*War Cross and Other Texts*], will captivate the general reader, his many reflections on colonial and post-colonial culture and history, as well as Goan literature, will attract the scholar's attention since, in the same way that he brings together different narrative genres, he crosses geographical and cultural boundaries to depict the figure of the Portuguese and Goan returnees from the wars of independence in Africa, to portray the life of the dwindling Goan diasporic population in Lisbon, to offer glimpses of Salazar's Portugal from a fresh angle and, principally, to tell stories about life in Goa before and after the Indian takeover in 1961. Also, he analyses the works of some of the most outstanding Goan writers in Portuguese, such as Vimala Devi and Maria Elsa da Rocha, or in English, like Selma Carvalho. In his mosaic of narratives, which directly or indirectly refer to different moments of Rocha's own life, lived between Goa and Portugal, fictional accounts have the power of historiography while the retelling of historical facts becomes as engrossing as fictional narratives.

While 'Cruz de Guerra' [War Cross] and 'A Morte do Lulu' [Lulu Dies Alone] are two of the most remarkable short stories in the collection, 'Conversa com Leopoldo' [A Talk with Leopoldo], based on an interview published in the Portuguese journal *Triângulo* (2016), is an outstanding autobiographical piece. Many of the questions posed by the journalist António Vieira would eventually receive a full answer in the novel *Casa Grande: recordações de um velho goês* [*Casa Grande: Memories of an Old Goan*] published in Lisbon in 2008. One of the interview's highlights is Rocha's reflection that the Portuguese-speaking Goan diaspora, i.e. the Goan diaspora in Portugal whose mother tongue was Portuguese, was slowly disappearing and being eclipsed by what he defines as a diaspora of English expression, in other words, the children of Goan expatriates to Portuguese and British colonies in Africa or the Gulf who later on moved to English-speaking countries. He argues that, while there are many records of the diaspora in English, there are almost none of the diaspora in Portuguese. He feels that he is part of this memory. He sees himself as a character of this past history not only because he lived in colonial Goa, and was part of the Catholic gentry, but because he was also there when Goa was annexed to India, and later on when the Portuguese language ceased to have any official standing in Goa. Yet, as he takes pains to emphasize, he himself continued to write in Portuguese no matter what. In other words, he himself is a living memory of that time. The fear that there might be no records of this world fast receding into the past might be one of the main reasons that led him to compile in a book the many pieces that make up this collection and that, as he says in the Preamble, were scattered in the web. Nonetheless, as the subtitle to the interview 'Memórias que podem causar desconforto' [Memories that Might Cause Discomfort] suggests, Rocha's recollections caused much uproar, not only when the interview was published but also when they found full expression in *Casa Grande*, as he has no qualms about criticizing the Catholic gentry's shortcomings, such as their defence of the caste system or their critique of the Hindu community. Likewise, as also transpires in other parts of *Cruz de Guerra*, as much as he admires the Jesuits' intellectuality and their love of knowledge, he is very harsh on the vow of celibacy. Himself forced to enter the seminary at the age of ten, Rocha, the son of landowners, abandoned the cloth when he moved to Portugal.

As with most of Rocha's narratives, *Cruz de Guerra* peers into his own past, which is entwined with that of Goans both outstanding and ordinary, both at home and abroad. Though his viewpoint is far from romantic or sentimental — at one point he describes Goan Freedom Fighters breaking into his ageing parents' great house to steal a gun — and he is highly critical of Goans, he is determined to narrate episodes that show Goans at their best. One such example would be the undeniable link between the Hindus and the Catholics, as the final piece in the book, 'Recordando uns episódios em Goa: tempo português em viragem' [Remembering some Goan Episodes: Changing Portuguese Times], attests. It recounts the author's experience in the Seminar of Rachol, the heart of Catholicism in Goa, when Rabindranath Tagore's play *Sanyassi*, on Hindu philosophy, was performed. Another example would be his love of local customs and Goa's language, Konkani, when he chooses to narrate that on the same occasion, in that same temple of erudition, where mostly Latin was spoken, a young Christian from Mardol got up on stage and, in the style of the popular *tyatr*, delivered a monologue about the vicissitudes of a cowherd when an ox runs away from the herd to go after a cow! What makes *Cruz de Guerra* a page-turner is Rocha's ability to switch not only between genres and topics, but also between narrative tones. If he can be severely critical, he can also be amusing and entertaining.

MANUEL CLEMENTE, *O que é Portugal? O que somos e porque o somos* (Lisbon: Universidade Católica Editora, 2015), 45 pages. Print.

PEDRO GARCIA MARQUES, *O segredo da justiça* (Lisbon: Universidade Católica Editora, 2016), 75 pages. Print.

ISABEL CAPELOA GIL, *Humanidade(s): considerações radicalmente contemporâneas* (Lisbon: Universidade Católica Editora, 2016), 60 pages + bibliography and notes. Print.

HANS ULRICH GUMBRECHT, *A Filologia e o Presente*, trans. by Ana Maria Carneiro (Lisbon: Universidade Católica Editora, 2017), 50 pages + notes. Print.

ANNETTE BONGARDT AND FRANCISCO TORRES, *Brexit: uma questão de racionalidade política* (Lisbon: Universidade Católica Editora, 2017), 46 pages + notes. Print.

Reviewed by PAULO DE MEDEIROS, University of Warwick

In 2015 the Press of the Catholic University of Portugal (UCP) started a new series, with the title of Argumentos, which now includes twenty-five books, the latest of which is devoted to sacred art and architecture in Braga. Although the Press (Universidade Católica Editora) has been publishing for twenty years in a diverse range of academic fields and disciplines, including not only the Humanities and Social Sciences but also Law, Business, Engineering and Theology, it does not enjoy much visibility outside those fields. The new series could change that, as it is interdisciplinary, very topical and accessible. Published in cooperation with the Fundação Cupertino de Miranda and priced at five euros per volume (€4.50 initially), there are many reasons for it to become a success and reach a wider audience beyond the restricted groves of academia. Unlike the comparable series published directly by the Fundação Cupertino de Miranda — also very topical and priced even lower, with the paperback versions costing just three euros — which is widely available to the general public in special displays placed in most supermarkets as well as bookstores, this series still needs better distribution if it is ultimately to reach the wide audience it addresses in Portugal. Conversely — and this is both unusual and very welcome — the books can be purchased from Amazon UK for a still modest five pounds plus postage. The topics covered are wide-ranging, encompassing some questions more restricted to an academic interest while others speak to anyone wishing to be informed, be it on euthanasia, the question of Europe, or the impact of refugees. Some of the topics covered by these little books — averaging fifty pages each in a comfortable format between A6 and A5, complemented by an attractive and simple cover in varying uniform colours — are portentous but the series also embraces humour and it is a pleasant surprise to see that one of the 2017 books was a translation of Swift's sermon 'Upon Sleeping in Church'. The five books here under review could be said to offer a sampling of the series, with a focus on questions directly related to the Humanities and written, with one exception, by Portuguese authors.

The series' inaugural volume, Manuel Clemente's *O que é Portugal? O que somos e porque o somos* is appropriately symptomatic as it reflects the country's perennial preoccupation with its national identity. The initial occasion for the essay was the acceptance speech proffered by its author, both as historian and as Cardinal Patriarch of Lisbon, on the occasion of receiving the Prémio Pessoa in 2009. As such, it seems clear that more than just finding an outlet for the text the Catholic University wished to mark its new series with a reflection on cultural identity that was traditional as well as open to the future. The very conclusion of the essay could be called in as evidence of this, referencing the famed *História do Futuro* by Padre António Vieira and at the same time decrying both rancid delusions of imperialism and facile defeatism. This is a rational, sober view of Portugal as a small nation within the larger context of European and indeed world events. It is also a positive belief in the possibilities offered for the future as long as the people, in this case, the Portuguese, decide to work towards realizing them. Although such a view could be seen as banal in itself, perhaps even a little trite, it should be read in the light of the world financial crisis in 2007 and 2008 and, of course, Portugal's own financial crisis that led to the intervention of the IMF and EU and the imposition of catastrophic austerity measures in 2010. Without straying too far from the centre, or indeed from a traditional view of the country's historical significance, the discourse on Portugal put forward in this essay starts, significantly, from a questioning and ironic view of empire and Portugal's assumed teleological destiny as a 'civilizational force in Africa'. The opening extended citation from the conclusion to Eça de Queirós's *Ilustre Casa de Ramires* forms the appropriate backdrop and source for the author's resolute rejection of any such notions of predestination for empire or whatever, without, in any way, giving in to the cultural pessimism and inferiority complexes that for so long, since Eça's time, have haunted Portugal.

Arguably, Pedro Garcia Marques's *O segredo da justiça* has the most seductive title. Its contents, however, are more mixed and, in spite of a serious attempt at a prose not without literary qualities, a bit drier, which is not a bad thing on the whole. The topic is very timely of course — indeed, one has only to follow the recent news on 'Operation Lex' concerning corruption in the world of sports, politics and the judicial system itself, to understand its urgency — and has wider implications for an understanding of our current political situation and the way in which it threatens the very foundations of what had been assumed as unassailable institutional guarantees for democracy and the rule of law in Western societies. To a certain extent the initial quotation from Kafka's *The Trial* is misleading in so far as the matter in question is not so much the hiding of evidence from the accused, who, like K. would not even know what he was being charged with, but rather the lack of disclosure of case elements that might harm the alleged victims or prevent the successful completion of the investigative process. Of course, the issues are complex and to maintain a balance between attempts to safeguard the innocent and the transparency demanded by a democratic society is often to walk a tightrope. Although this book is perhaps more directly aimed at colleagues in legal theory than the average reader, its aim is a very important one.

The Humanities are ostensibly the topic of both Isabel Capeloa Gil's and Hans Ulrich Gumbrecht's books, yet that is where the similarities end. If one wanted to look for a way to illustrate the weaknesses and strengths of a collection like this, these two books would be an almost ideal odd couple. It is tempting to keep in this vein and try to impute a certain fatalistic pessimism inherent in what would be a spent form of criticism that seems to pervade the essay Gumbrecht first published in English in 2015 ('Philology and the Complex Present' in *Florilegium* (2015), 273–81), and which is at the base of the current book in Portuguese translation. But that would be to simplify, even falsify, Gumbrecht's position. For although he spends most of the space going over historical considerations, his conclusion is not (or, in any case, not only) a hopeless plea for a return to classical philology and the rigours of scholarship, even if the largely unnecessary anecdote concerning the PhD candidate still using an obsolete critical edition of a particular text would seem to point that way. Rather, Gumbrecht is very much aware of, and interested in, newer technological developments and the possibilities they can hold for a renewal of the Humanities. It is in this light that he references, however briefly, Franco Moretti's project involving big data and 'distant reading' as well as Digital Humanities in general. Gumbrecht is obviously an influential comparatist and a keen observer of the fads and vagaries of literary studies, whose impressive scope and lifelong intellectual engagement often make for compelling reading. The present argument, however, in a sense, goes all the way back — as he notes in passing — to his earlier book on *The Powers of Philology* (University of Illinois Press, 2003). It is not that there is not much to be learned there, but what I find more difficult is that the intrusion of societal issues into the hallowed world of scholarship, in spite of Gumbrecht's own call for an attention to embodiment, can be held so magnificently at bay. Interestingly enough, part of the book is actually a dialogue between Isabel Capeloa Gil and Hans Ulrich Gumbrecht, where their divergent views on the current state of the Humanities can be glimpsed through all the courtesies of polite dialogue. To some readers that brief exchange might well prove to hold more relevant questions than the essay that precedes it and some might even wish they had jumped to it straight away, even knowing that it would then, perhaps, not be properly understood.

Isabel Capeloa Gil, who was invested as Rector of the Catholic University in the Fall of 2016, has written one of the most incisive books in the series, directed certainly at fellow Humanists — a comparatist, she is Professor of Culture Studies — but reaching to a wider educated audience. The book, conceived, as she says right at the start, as 'more than a simple rhetorical flourish and certainly as a provocation' (p. 7), is an important reflection on the Humanities, their fundamental role in society, their key concerns and their infinite state of crisis which, rather than being new or incidental, can be said to be one of the Humanities' defining characteristics. Crucially, she identifies the growing discourse of disaffection with the attacks on traditional aspects of the Humanities and even on the hypothetical value the Humanities might still hold in a profoundly consumerist society such as ours as jeremiads, best left behind if we are to seriously engage with the challenges today's world poses for the Humanities. As such it could not perhaps be more neatly opposed to Gumbrecht's book. For Gil the role and function of the Humanities cannot be conceived in opposition to society at large, much less in avoidance of it. Universities have a clear goal in educating and preparing successive generations to continue working not only to keep tradition but to enable it to persevere by adapting it. This is no philistine or simply opportunistic position but rather one that is both enriched by Gil's formidable scholarship in several areas from classical literature to German studies, from performance studies to visual culture — all of which in a limited way come to bear on her argument — and by her wide experience with the practicalities of funding and assessment at various national and international levels. One way in which to read the 'radical contemporaneous' of her subtitle is to see her position as fundamentally rejecting any nostalgic investment in the past, drawing fully from it but above all preoccupied with the privileged position of the Humanities, not merely as keepers of tradition but, above all, as keepers of the polity, in a direct reference to the report *The Heart of the Matter*, published by the American Academy of Arts & Sciences: 'As we strive to create a more civil public discourse, a more adaptable and creative workforce, and a more secure nation, the humanities and social sciences are the heart of the matter, the keeper of the republic' (2013, p. 9).

This same view that the Humanities and Social Sciences should cast a critical eye on society and contribute not just to the upholding of ideals, but also to the safeguarding of basic rights, is at the base of the discussion on Brexit co-authored by Annette Bongardt and Fernando Torres, both social scientists with a research record on European affairs and with direct experience of Britain, among other countries, as visiting fellows at the London School of Economics. The argument in itself could not be simpler: Brexit would be the logical result of growing divergences between the perceived interests of the UK and the EU, divergences that had always interfered with the UK's full participation in the programme of the EU. Regardless of whether one agrees or not with such a view, the book is both predictable and surprising. It is surprising of course, because it might have seemed unthinkable, before 23 June 2016, that a core member of the EU and one of its motors, would decide to leave the EU with all the complexity, and risk, such a move entails. Yet it is exactly against such a notion of surprise that the book lays out evidence that should have led political analysts, at least, to expect such a result. As they suggest, 'the United Kingdom was always opposed to the model (necessarily political) of European integration' (p. 9). It is predictable though, as the view it takes, inasmuch as it draws on knowledge of the political and economic specificities of the United Kingdom, must ultimately be said to be a continental one. This becomes very evident in the book's logical conclusion that, given circumstances, once the United Kingdom has finally achieved its goal of leaving the European Union, the European Union will gain as, freed from a dissenting voice, it can proceed much more systematically towards the aimed-for integration. One might think that a book on such a topic would be out of date before even being published. That this is not at all the case has less to do with the near glacial speed (before climate change) at which negotiations between the UK and the EU have been moving, than with the fact that the historical analysis is every bit as important as the considerations of what might happen to the European Union the day after Brexit. It is a tempting little book, if for nothing else than for the very engagement with such a fundamental question for the future of all of us in Europe that tries to steer clear of ideological pitfalls. And yet, one might also think that, far from being a rational and logical conclusion, Brexit is one more, albeit extreme, example of how populism has radically changed all our lives and entrenched beliefs. At stake then, as D. Manuel Clemente, Pedro Garcia Marques and Isabel Capeloa Gil also variously imply, is the need to work from within the Humanities and Social Sciences to resist such fundamental threats to democracy, made all the more sinister when cloaked in the appearance of a fetishized and imaginary 'will of the people'.

Abstracts

What 25 April Was and Why It Mattered
Robert M. Fishman

Abstract. This article takes up the conceptual question of how to understand the Carnation Revolution that commenced on 25 April 1974 and the related historical question of the enduring consequences of Portugal's distinctive pathway from dictatorship to democracy. The central argument emphasizes the multiple and overlapping meanings of 25 April: as a liberating coup that ended decades of anti-democratic rule, as the beginning of a transition to democracy, as the foundation for a social revolution that would overturn multiple institutional hierarchies and reconfigure cultural phenomena, and finally as a precondition for a subsequent turn to socialist revolution. The historically unusual intertwining of these analytically distinct processes has provided 25 April with a significance that is reflected not only in the positive legacies to be found within Portugal but also in the contributions of this national case to the inauguration of an ultimately worldwide wave of democratization.
Keywords. 25 April, Carnation Revolution, democratization, social revolution, Portugal.

Resumo. Este artigo aborda a questão conceptual de como compreender a Revolução dos Cravos, que teve início a 25 de abril de 1974, e a questão histórica relacionada com as consequências duradouras do caminho distintivo de Portugal, da ditadura até à democracia. O argumento central enfatiza os significados múltiplos e sobrepostos de 25 de abril: enquanto um golpe libertador que encerrou décadas de governo antidemocrático, como o início de uma transição para a democracia, como base para uma revolução social que iria subverter múltiplas hierarquias institucionais e reconfigurar fenómenos culturais e, finalmente, como pré-condição para subsequente revolução socialista. O intercâmbio historicamente raro destes processos analiticamente distintos atribui ao 25 de abril um significado que se reflete não apenas nos legados positivos que se encontram em Portugal, mas também na contribuição deste caso nacional para a inauguração de uma onda de democratização ao nível mundial.
Palavras-chave. 25 de Abril, democratização, Revolução dos Cravos, revolução social, Portugal.

Constitution-Making and the Democratization of Portugal: An Enduring Legacy
ANTÓNIO COSTA PINTO

ABSTRACT. Portuguese democratic transition in the 1970s produced one of the most left-wing constitutions of the Third Wave of democratization. The aim of this article is to explain the apparent puzzle of how an elected Constitutional Assembly dominated by the moderate right and left, with a Communist minority, produced a constitution closer to the principles of the latter. This had an almost immediate consequence: with the consolidation of democracy, the most committed defenders of the constitution were those who lost the political struggle during the most radical phase of Portuguese democratization, especially the Communists.

KEYWORDS. Constitutions, democratization, Constitutional Assembly, Portugal.

RESUMO. A transição para a democracia em Portugal nos anos 70 produziu uma das Constituições mais à esquerda das democratizações da terceira vaga. O objetivo deste artigo é explicar o aparente puzzle de uma Assembleia Constituinte dominada pela esquerda e direita moderadas, com uma minoria comunista, ter produzido uma Constituição mais próxima dos valores desta última. Esta característica teve uma consequência quase imediata: com a consolidação democrática, os mais ardorosos defensores da Constituição foram os que perderam a batalha durante a fase mais radical da democratização portuguesa, especialmente os comunistas.

PALAVRAS-CHAVE. Constituições, democratização, Assembleia Constituinte, Portugal.

The Cooperative Movement in Portugal beyond the Revolution: Housing Cooperatives between Shifting Tides
CAMILA RODRIGUES AND TIAGO FERNANDES

ABSTRACT. This article analyses the development of the housing cooperative movement in Portugal from the 1974 revolution to the present day. It is driven by the desire to answer historically grounded questions concerned with the impact of the democratization process and the democratic experience in the path taken by Portuguese cooperatives. As such, the study deals with particular issues rather than large-scale structures, processes and patterns of change and does not aim to make broad generalizations. The strategy is essentially interpretive, since the main focus is on the culturally determined intentions of the agents involved in the process, gathered through interviews with relevant actors and documental analysis.

KEYWORDS. Cooperative movement, housing, revolution, democracy, Portugal.

RESUMO. O ensaio analisa o desenvolvimento do movimento cooperativo no setor habitacional em Portugal, desde a revolução de 1974 até ao presente.

A sua força motriz reside no desejo de responder a questões historicamente situadas relativas ao impacto do processo de democratização e da experiência democrática no percurso das cooperativas portuguesas; logo, aborda questões particulares e não estruturas, processos e padrões gerais de mudança. Como tal, a pesquisa não apresenta ambições significativas de generalização. A estratégia é essencialmente interpretativa, uma vez que o foco principal reside nas intenções culturalmente determinadas dos agentes envolvidos captadas mediante entrevistas a atores relevantes no processo e análise documental.
PALAVRAS-CHAVE. Movimento cooperativo, habitação, revolução, democracia, Portugal.

The Portuguese Presidencies of the European Union: A Preliminary Study
NUNO SEVERIANO TEIXEIRA AND REINALDO SARAIVA HERMENEGILDO

ABSTRACT. Portugal has held the Presidency of the Council on three separate occasions: 1992, 2000, and 2007. These terms correspond to different phases in the European integration process and to different Portuguese positions with respect to European integration. In the three contexts, this article analyses the presidencies on three different levels: the definition of their political programmes and priorities, the organization of the diplomatic machinery and the management of various dossiers, and an assessment of the results obtained, from the perspective of Portuguese foreign policy and in terms of its impact on the European process. The article argues that in the case of a small- or medium-sized power such as Portugal, the presidential term has an even greater relevance: firstly, because (in contrast to its significance for larger powers) the presidency represents a unique opportunity to influence, if not to lead, the European agenda; and secondly, because at certain moments in negotiations, weakness can be a strength, meaning that a small power might more easily achieve agreement and consensus among the great powers.
KEYWORDS. Council of the European Union, foreign policy, Portugal, presidency.

RESUMO. Portugal ocupou a Presidência do Conselho em três ocasiões: 1992, 2000 e 2007. Estes momentos corresponderam a diferentes fases do processo de integração europeia e a diferentes posições portuguesas em relação à integração europeia. Nos três contextos, no artigo são analisadas as Presidências em três níveis diferentes: a definição dos programas e prioridades políticas, a organização da máquina diplomática e a gestão dos vários processos, e uma avaliação dos resultados obtidos, a partir da perspetiva portuguesa de política externa e em termos de seu impacto no processo europeu. No artigo é argumentado que, no caso de um poder de pequena ou média dimensão, como Portugal, o mandato presidencial tem ainda maior relevância: em primeiro lugar, porque (em contraste com a sua importância para os poderes de maior dimensão) a Presidência representa uma oportunidade única para influenciar a agenda europeia, se não mesmo para liderar; e em segundo lugar, porque em certos momentos da negociação, a fraqueza pode ser um ponto forte, o que significa que um pequeno poder pode mais facilmente chegar a um acordo e a um consenso entre as grandes potências.

PALAVRAS-CHAVE. Conselho da União Europeia, política externa, Portugal, Presidência.

The Legacies of Revolution: Path-Dependence and Economic Performance in Portugal
SEBASTIÁN ROYO

ABSTRACT. This article examines how Portugal's revolutionary legacies have affected the country's economic performance in the years prior to the global financial crisis, from 1999 to 2007. The main argument is that the distinctiveness of the country's pathway from dictatorship to democracy, coupled with other crucial features of its recent political past, helped to set the stage for the subsequent economic challenges that the country experienced following accession to European Monetary Union in 1999.

KEYWORDS. Portugal, economic policy, legacies of revolution, Carnation Revolution.

RESUMO. Este artigo examina como os legados revolucionários em Portugal afetaram o desempenho da economia nos anos que precederam a crise financeira global, de 1999 a 2007. O argumento principal apresentado é que o caráter distintivo da passagem do autoritarismo à democracia, associado a algumas características do seu passado político recente, ajudaram a criar as condições para os desafios subsequentes que o País conheceu a seguir à adesão à União Económica e Monetária em 1999.

PALAVRAS-CHAVE. Portugal, política económica, legados da revolução, Revolução dos Cravos.

Portugal's Social and Labour Market Policy: The Crisis, the Troika and Beyond
MIGUEL GLATZER

ABSTRACT. Starting in 2009, Portugal was hit hard by the Eurozone crisis. This article provides an overview of the effects of the crisis, and the policy responses to it, on Portuguese unemployment, poverty, inequality and emigration. It then examines the changes in social and labour market policy that were externally imposed by the Troika through its emphasis on austerity and structural reform. Finally, it evaluates the partial reversals undertaken by the António Costa government, arguing that these were made possible by (1) the end of the memorandums of understanding, (2) Portugal's success in reducing its budget deficit, and (3) the new nature of EU supervision under the European Semester system. In examining policies on the labour market, pensions, the minimum wage and anti-poverty programmes, the article argues that these policy areas have undergone distinct shifts in governance from broad national autonomy, to strict external control, to relative autonomy as long as budget deficit targets are met.

KEYWORDS. Portugal, crisis, employment, social policies, Troika.

RESUMO. Começando em 2009, a crise do euro teve impactos fortes em Portugal. Este artigo descreve os efeitos da crise, e das consequentes respostas políticas, nas taxas de desemprego, pobreza, desigualdade e emigração. O artigo examina as reformas das políticas sociais e do emprego impostas sobre Portugal consoante o ênfase na austeridade e as reformas estruturais da Troika. Finalmente, o artigo analisa as reversões parciais realizadas pelo governo de António Costa. Estas inversões tornaram-se possíveis devido (1) ao fim dos memorandos, (2) o sucesso de Portugal na redução do défice orçamental, e (3) a nova natureza de supervisão da União Europeia enquadrada no programa do Semestre Europeu. Examinando as políticas de emprego, pensões, salário mínimo e do combate à pobreza, este artigo argumenta que nos últimos anos vemos três regimes de governação que as regulam: nomeadamente de autonomia nacional, de controle externo estrito, e de autonomia relativa desde que haja controle do défice orçamental.

PALAVRAS-CHAVE. Portugal, crise, políticas sociais, emprego, Troika.

www.ingramcontent.com/pod-product-compliance
Lightning Source LLC
Chambersburg PA
CBHW061417300426
44114CB00015B/1968